GOD'S INTENTION FOR MAN

Essays in Christian Anthropology

by

WILLIAM O. FENNELL

SUPPLEMEⁱ

GOD'S INTENTION FOR MAN

Essays in Christian Anthropology

by

WILLIAM O. FENNELL

SUPPLEMENTS / 4

GOD'S INTENTION FOR MAN

ESSAYS IN CHRISTIAN ANTHROPOLOGY

by

WILLIAM O. FENNELL

Canadian Cataloguing in Publication Data

Fennell, William O., 1916-
 God's intention for man

(SR supplements ; 4)

Contains the Warfield lectures delivered at Princeton
Theological Seminary in 1974.

ISBN 0-919812-05-8 pa.

1. Man (Theology) - Addresses, essays, lectures.
I. Title. II. Series.

BT703.F45   233   C77-001308-2

The Canadian Corporation for Studies in Religion is proud to present in its series SR Supplements this work of one of Canada's recognized leading theologians. For decades, William Fennell has not only touched the lives of ministers during their years of theological education but has been an actively sought out partner in theological discussion in this country, a discussion he helped shape. It was a fitting tribute to him that he was invited to be a Warfield Lecturer of Princeton Theological Seminary.

That Professor Fennell consented to have those lectures published by this Corporation as a part of its fledgling monograph series, is a source of great satisfaction to us. Our aim, to publish a journal and other scholarly material in the field of the scientific study of religion in order to serve the needs of scholars working in both the English and French languages in Canada, is fulfilled further by the opportunity to present this work to an 'audience' greater now than the original hearers of these lectures in Princeton.

Martin Rumscheidt
President
Canadian Corporation for
Studies in Religion

"When God created man, he made him in the likeness of God. Male and female he created them, and he blessed them and named them Man when they were created." Genesis 5: 1b-2

TABLE OF CONTENTS

INTRODUCTION

This book contains, almost without change in content or style, the Annie Kinkead Warfield Lectures delivered at Princeton Theological Seminary in February, 1974. It was a great honour to be the first Canadian invited to offer lectures in this distinguished series and a great relief to have my trepidations at being so eased by the appreciative reception given them by President James McCord and the members of the seminary community. I am indeed grateful for their friendly hospitality.

The theme of the lectures has been well worked over by contemporary theologians from almost every conceivable angle of Christian thought. Yet the subject was chosen because of a) a life-long personal interest in it; b) a deep conviction about its primary significance for Christian understanding and life; c) the disquiet and challenge that lay in the fact that though many in our day have spoken on the subject none seems to say things I find it necessary to say in order to achieve wholeness in Christian thought and life. Where the weaknesses and failures in my own attempt at understanding are to be found others will, I am sure, assist me to discover.

I approach the subject as a theologian of the Word of God. We speak in the title of God's intention for man thereby testifying that God is a being most appropriately witnessed to as Personal Will, one whose will is known to man. Our belief in this regard is formed and informed by the biblical witness to revelation which continues in some persuasive way to ring true. One finds himself still constrained to affirm the faith that comes from the hearing of the Gospel, witnessed to in scripture and received and interpreted by the community that it creates and sustains. It is my view that the Gospel of the self-revealed God still has power to convict and convince when faithfully witnessed. Development and renewal in Christian understanding occur when the truth of the Gospel is addressed by questions that arise both within the believing community and out of its encounter with the culture of our day. There is here, I suppose, a kind of theology of correlation. But it is a correlation that finds priority not in human assertions or questionings, ordered by no matter what philosophical, sociological and psychological principles of human understanding, but in a Gospel whose truth shines in its own light. However, before the salvation that Gospel offers is fulfilled in man, it must, in terms of understanding, be brought into correlation with every truth belonging to human life, and filled out with everything that makes life human in the world. In other words, there must be room in Christian thought for a dialectic of human question and divine answer, but the dialectic must take place within the context of an affirmation of God that transcends all self-originating human questioning. Christian theology is the account one gives of the truth that total process yields. I offer here a personal account of the present stage of my own believing affirmation and reflective questioning concerning the subject of God's intention for man.

I must confess to being somewhat troubled, as the reader may be too, by the fact that accents may seem to fall from time to time too heavily on man in essays that purport to be essays in theology. Karl Barth confessed that in his theology, particularly in the early part, man's voice may have been somewhat drowned out in the thunder of his speech about God. We may be running here a risk in the opposite direction. But we do so paradoxically, only in order to speak rightly about man as seen from the perspective of God and his gracious intention.

It will soon become evident that what is attempted here is nothing in the way of a system, even in outline, of dogmatic understanding of the Christian faith. As has been suggested above, what dictates the subject matter discussed is most often some of the questions addressed to faith in current theological discussion. Many traditional questions in the area of Christology, Soteriology and the Christian Life remain untouched, and many others receive but a glancing reference. But in theology the whole is reflected in the part and the part must be tested by its fidelity to the whole.

One final word concerning style. As a systematic theologian I have been somewhat troubled by elements of repetition that have found their way into the various sections of the book and that I have allowed to remain there. Normally, I suppose, theology isn't done this way. But perhaps a small, compact series of this sort allows for the assertion and reassertion of a theme, of sub-themes and variations on the theme. T. S. Eliot, to whom we are indebted for a major reference in the book, once wrote an extended poem in a style that warranted the title "Four Quartettes". Is it ever justified to do theology in a somewhat, even if distantly, similar fashion? In any event, that is the consoling rationalization I offer for the repetitions that occur from time to time of which the reader must become aware. Perhaps Dr. Warfield, as a Professor of Didactic and Polemic Theology, would not have minded too much.

CHAPTER 1

THE ARROW OF FAITH

A basic conviction of these lectures is that many Christian thinkers have the arrow of faith's understanding of God pointed in the wrong direction. The reason for this lies mainly, I suppose, in the continuing influence of Greek philosophical thought on contemporary as well as traditional modes of Christian understanding. Even theologians who are otherwise critical of that influence continue to show it in this regard at least. The direction of the flight of the arrow of faith under its influence is represented by the term "transcendence". God is thought of as transcendent reality, the above and beyond, toward which all nature points and toward whom man is thought rightly to aspire. The pathway of faith is thought to lead out of time into eternity, from finitude to participation in the infinity of God. Both Roman Catholic and Protestant theologians of great stature, whose thought is otherwise at crucial points diverse and even contradictory, share in common something of this *tendenz.* They develop Christian anthropologies of virtual or implied deification that view man's final destiny as being filled with the being of God. God wills to be "all in all", in himself and in all else besides. Man has been created with that end in mind. "Thou hast made us for thyself", says St. Augustine, "and our hearts are restless until they find their rest in thee." There may indeed be ways of understanding this confession, as we shall see, that do not distort God's intention for man as I have come to understand it. But very often it is interpreted by Christian theologians in ways that lead in an opposite direction to that believed by me to be willed by God. From their perspective the calling addressed by God to man, whom he has made for himself alone, leads away from any conception of finite existence fulfilled in terms of finite goodness, to a conception of a human existence that is finally good only when filled without remainder with the goodness of God.

I give an example first from a source to which very often I am happy to refer in total agreement. Karl Barth, quite early in his *Church Dogmatics* says about human speech: "Not all man's language is language about God. *Perhaps it really might and ought to be.* In principle, we can give no reason for it being otherwise."[1] Barth then goes on to say that in man's natural state and in the state of glory "all his language is language about God." If I have not misunderstood him, Barth here at least thinks and speaks about man "religiously". God wills to be for man in actuality the sum total of the content of his being as man. Man's relation to God seems to exhaust the meaning of his humanity. There is finally room for nothing other than deity if the reality of God is exclusively the subject of man's speech and thus presumably of his thought. Later on in the *Dogmatics*, perhaps under

1

influences that led to the writing of the pamphlet on the *Humanity of God* Barth says something that I find quite different. Here he says:

> "In themselves and as such (human) speaking and hearing are a wonderful possibility in the realization of which the human situation could and should and would become *really human*. What should take place in human speaking and hearing is the utterance, declaration and revelation of *human reality* with a view to its indication, impartation and communication to others and with the *final purpose* of the communion or fellowship of the one with the others."[2]

Here the arrow of faith is indeed turned in another direction. Not now human destiny viewed "religiously", God filling up the totality of human thought and speech. Rather, God calling and setting man free for a life filled with finite goodness, "fellowship in human reality" thought of as a *final goal* of speech.

As a second example of a misdirected arrow of faith, I choose Karl Rahner. Rahner, in a remarkable work on natural theology, expands the view that man can by reason be shown to be essentially a "Hearer of the Word of God".[3] In his natural state he is a listener for the Word of God. Who God is whom he has been created to hear, and what God will say to man cannot be known naturally. God must first speak for that reality in truth to be known. Still, God has made man for himself: (a) a being by nature who is an unceasing *listener* for the voice of God, if God has not spoken; (b) a finite hearer of the Word of God if and when God wills to speak. For Christian man God indeed has spoken, supremely in the human history of the incarnate Son.

Here too, as he develops this theme along with others, there seems to be no theological reason why man's language should be any other than language about God when human nature has arrived at its God-willed destiny. For Rahner too the fulfilment of the humanity of man lies in believing reception of the Word of God — and that (and this is the significant point!) without remainder. In the development of Karl Barth's theology there is not, of course, as there is in Rahner's, any conception of human destiny as ontic participation in deity through the union of God with man accomplished first in Jesus Christ. Indeed in Barth, as theologian of the Word of God, there is a more consistent development of Rahner's understanding of man as made to be a hearer of God's Word. By grace alone, through faith alone, man is by the enablement of God's spirit made to be a hearer, in a finite mode of hearing, of the eternal conversation of God with God. For both theologians there is, in principle now, and finally in reality, no reason why human language should be any other than a language formed and informed by God's word.

Our third example is Paul Tillich. For all the vast differences otherwise, he shares with Barth and Rahner this "religious" understanding of man's nature and destiny viewed from the perspective of God. For him, too, man is one essentially made for God. He like all finite being has proceeded from God. To the extent that he has being, he participates in God. To the extent that he is finite, he participates in non-being as well. So God is regarded by Tillich as man's "lost infinity", one with whom man's eschatological destiny is once more to be fully one when, non-being conquered by being, God will be all in all.[4]

I beg the reader's indulgence for this sketchy and inadequate account of examples of Christian anthropology that seem clearly to interpret the nature and destiny of man "religiously". The reformed tradition asks the question: "What is the chief end of man?" And answers: "Man's chief end is to glorify God and enjoy him forever." I regard this confession of faith to be incontrovertibly true. But I do not think that its truth is rightly interpreted when it is interpreted "religiously". There may be another possibility, more in keeping with God's intention for man as made known in the scripture's witness to revelation. To glorify God means to understand and to order life entirely in accord with His revealed will. And the enjoyment of God forever may, as Barth also testified, include the enjoyment of our humanity when it is rightly ordered by the reality and truth of God.

One will have gathered from the foregoing that by a "religious" understanding of human nature and destiny I mean one that views man not only essentially but exclusively in terms of the God-ward reference of his being. A religious understanding[5] would regard any deflection of human thought and interest toward "other-than-God" either as a temporary and excusable aberration due to the conditions of finitude, or an inexcusable sign of sin. Such religious longing and aspiration may be found in the well-know hymn:

> "God be in my head and in my understanding;
> God be in my eyes and in my looking;
> God be in my mouth, and in my speaking ..."[6]

There are times in Christian life when such an aspiration is most appropriate — in particular, as we shall see, times of worship and meditation. It does indeed express an attitude and aspiration *central* to one's being as man. But as an expression of faith's understanding of Christian life as a whole it does not tell the whole truth of what God wills for us in the fulfilment of our humanity.

The question that arises here is not the pragmatic one whether under earthly conditions of life such a longing could with utmost seriousness be intended or whether even in the most saintly fashion it could ever be fulfilled. Nor is it the interesting "psychology of religion" question, if one *does* let God into life, how is it possible not to be solely absorbed by him? The really serious question is the *theological* question, whether such a religious understanding of life is in accord with God's purpose for man. It is true that in his self-revealing Word that culminates in Jesus some things are said that bear close relation to things about which we have been speaking. But other things are said which give them an orientation different from that found in the examples cited. It is this orientation I wish briefly to explore.

Let us straightway confess that in his Word God declares his will to be both at the centre and the circumference of human life. The alternative to a "religious" understanding is not a "secularist" understanding in which man is thought to be only, *or even primarily* related to what is "other-than-God". There are modern theologies in contrast to the ones cited above that seem to go in this latter direction, where God is thought of solely as means to human ends or where the term God is used to represent the dynamics of human personhood. We must assert the error of all such views even though they may be heretical, or even apostate, ways of seeking to do justice to an understanding of God's will for man that the so-called religious views have neglected or misunderstood. God as supreme personal reality can never rightfully be thought of simply as means to any end! To reduce the meaning of his being as some seem to do to some transcendent principle of relativity or to use the term God simply as a way of expressing hidden, mysterious, unknown sources of grace for freedom in human life, is to deny to God his God-ness and to make him simply tangential to human existence in utterly false ways.

I wish now to sketch in outline the direction in which I think the arrow of faith should be thought to fly as it follows faithfully God's revelation of himself and the truth of his intention for man.

God in Christian understanding, out of the gracious, self-giving love he in himself is, wills that there should be another kind of reality than himself. God thought, so to speak, outward from himself toward the world, the creaturely realm which he willed to create. No doubt God found and finds joy in the free expression of his creative powers that creation was and is. But revelation discloses that it is *love — agape love —* that informed God's intention to create. And agape love we know from him is love that "seeks not its own". God creates the world not for his own sake but for the world's sake. God did not create the world in order to have more room to be God in, for he is absolutely sufficient in himself. He created the world for its own being and fulfilment as world. This means that there is a finite level of goodness which can in principle be good as such and not only when it is filled with the Being of God. Though it has the power to be good only in the power to be that God gives it, he in fact gives it a power to be good at its own finite level of goodness, setting it free from himself for its own accomplishment. If the finite world were simply consequence of a fall, Being being all there is, God would indeed be the world's own lost infinity. He would indeed be not only the Reality by which the world is, but the Reality that the world is, in so much as it is. Or, if the world were simply made "for God", he would be the sole end toward which all finite being moves — its *raison d'être* lying solely in its intention and capacity to lead to God. But God's will and intention in creation are according to his Word quite otherwise. His will is that the world shall have a meaning and a purpose also in and for itself, though of course never *by* itself. God wills the world to stand as it were on its own feet, with a power for such standing that he unceasingly gives.

The chief of the creatures thus created by God is man, a body-soul being, made of the dust of the earth and spirit in the image of God. And man is not simply body-soul being, but bi-sexual being as well. Man is man-woman being, man and woman willed by God to be mates suited for one another, with languages of communication that were not ever intended to be languages that speak only about God. In our next lecture we will speak more fully about the being of man in terms of the intention of God. Here we wish simply to assert that God makes man not simply as a finite stage whereon to enact his being as God. Rather, in self-giving love he gives to man himself a theatre in which to enact the human meaning of his being as a creature among creaturely reality, a master under God of a world that God has made.

The direction of the arrow of faith as followed thus far, with the path of its flight determined by God's nature and will of love, is from God toward the world which God in love has made, not so much for his own as for his creature's sake. There is no way to argue from the biblical witness to revelation that the world comes into being simply as a fall away from God. Nor can it I think be rightfully argued that the world exists as means of man's ascent toward God. Not from the world to God but from God to the world is the direction faith's arrow was intended to fly. Therefore, we cannot accept Teilhard de Chardin's teaching about the evolutionary history of the ascent of Spirit through matter and man which, when united with the downward thrust of God into the world, reaches its fulfilment in the deification of the finite by the infinity of God.[7]

In the biblical witness to God in relation to creation, he is not found at the end of an evolutionary process of becoming, nor is he the name of the process itself. Rather he is God at the beginning, giving to an already realized creation its power to be. God is not the Reality arrived at, but the Reality of origin; not a transcendent mystery pulling man upward in a gradual process of deification, but a mystery of Presence, man's companion in the world, enabling man to be *human* as body-soul being, humanizing the world.

Now we have by no means finished our account of the flight of the arrow of faith outward from God toward the world in speaking of creation. For when man refused his vocation simply to be human in the world in fellowship with God, God continues in love to act redemptively in order to fulfil His original intention. Bernard Lonergan speaks of man's "proud content to be just a man".[8] The biblical witness to man's fall seems to view it otherwise. Man in pride refused his vocation to be "just a man"! He refused the humanistic vocation given by God. He willed to be *as God*! Yet God remained constant in his intention that man should simply be a creature made for a human creature's life in the world. To restore to man knowledge of and power to effect his lost vocation, God engaged in a salvation history that had its fulfilment in his own embodiment in a human life. Out of God's eternity into time, not thereby to transform time into eternity, but rather to fulfil God's intention for time. Here eternity, so to speak, becomes the servant of the fulfilment of time, not time the servant, the stepping-stone, the opening into eternity. How deeply into time the eternal God came in his effort to redeem time for what we shall have to speak of as a self-fulfilling destiny, is the story of the saving work of Jesus Christ — "who for us men and our salvation, came down from heaven, was made man; he suffered and died; he descended into hell." That indeed is faith's witness to the flight of the arrow of God's descent into the world. Then there follows resurrection and ascension into heaven.

The question now comes with logical necessity: do we not now at least have a change in the direction of the arrow's flight? Is there a parabola movement here marking man's destiny? — the descent of God into the world followed by the ascent of man into the eternity of God? Did God in this sense become what we are in order that we might become what he is? Is the end of *incarnation* then some form of deification? We are constrained to answer "No" to these questions. This is not the way I believe these realities for faith should be interpreted. Incarnation, crucifixion, resurrection, ascension and second coming — these words testify to God's action of Presence, forgiveness, renewal in which man is given again freedom for the fulfilment of worldly human life. Not incarnation, death and resurrection to initiate or fulfil purposes of deification; but incarnation, death and resurrection to fulfil God's original intention that man should have freedom to fulfil *creation's* potentiality for good. The hope that is offered to faith in the Gospel is not really that of a finitude filled like Jesus with the deity of God, man's humanity transcended in a beatitude wherein God's being is all in all. Rather, we are offered in God's Word for our hopeful believing the promise of a new heaven and a new earth wherein righteousness dwells, into which the nations will bring their glory, offering to God the harvest of human endeavour for his forgiving acceptance and wherein nature, freed from death and all that makes for death, will live and bring forth life in enduring splendour.[9]

In the chapters that follow we will seek to extend our theological understanding of this view of God's intention for man and to show something of its meaning and significance for present life and future hope. In this chapter we have sought simply to show that the arrow of faith that follows God's revealed intention for man flies in a constant direction outward from God toward the world, then into the world of his creating to rescue man from sin and death.

Karl Barth has said:

"It is by Him, Jesus Christ, and for Him and to Him that the universe is created as a theatre of God's dealings with man and man's dealing with God ... There is nothing that is not from Him and by Him and to Him."[10]

We affirm the truth of this statement as a witness to what it means to have God at the centre and circumference of human life. It is a truth which comes to most unambiguous expression in man's worship and service of God, and of that we shall attempt to speak. But we are constrained also to ask whether the quotation and Barth's theology as a whole, do full justice to the intention of God for man, in particular with regard to the freedom he gives, not for the fulfilment of *God's* humanity but for the fulfilment of man's own.

FOOTNOTES

1 Karl Barth, *Church Dogmatics*, Volume I, Part 1, Edinburgh, T. & T. Clark, 1936, p. 51.

2 Karl Barth, *op. cit.*, Volume IV, Part 3, pp. 472-3: italics mine.

3 Karl Rahner, *Hearers of the Word*, tr. by Michael Richards, New York, Herder and Herder, 1969.

4 cf. Paul Tillich, *Systematic Theology*, Vols. I-III, Chicago, Chicago University Press, 1951, 1957, 1963. Re. the concept of God as "man's lost infinity" see especially Tillich's article "A Reinterpretation of the Doctrine of Incarnation" in *Church Quarterly Review*, Volume 147, January-March, 1949. Interpreting this article in its own terms, and in view of the total Tillich corpus, it does not seem at all inaccurate to speak as we have done here. At first glance, it may seem not to do justice to the subtlety of the Tillichean dialectic between finitude and infinity in the concept of essential Godmanhood. However, when one unfolds the logic of (a) the identification of Being and God; (b) the transition from essence to existence, involving a "fall" in which are elements of necessity as well as freedom; (c) finitude constituted through participation in non-being as well as being; (d) Tillich's speaking in the *Review* article of *our* infinity and *our* eternity, and speaking as well of the inseparability of God and man, the statements we have made here would seem to have ample support. Interpreting Tillich is always difficult because the language used in speaking about essential Godmanhood as disclosed in the manifestation of the New Being in Jesus as the Christ under the conditions of existence, and therefore in terms of the problematic of that existence, seems sometimes at odds with the language he uses in speaking of essence

and existence in a philosophical context, or again, and more particularly, when he speaks within the eschatological framework of creation, fall and final fulfilment when "existence is overcome".

5   Later, in chapter 5, I will raise the question whether "religion" may not be a useful category to represent, in distinction from science, art and morality, man's account of his encounter with a mysterious, transcendent dimension of nature. In this latter case, its object is interpreted to be not God but world and therefore represents a view of religion quite different from the "religious view of life" we are describing here.

6   See, *inter alia, The Hymn Book* of the Anglican Church of Canada and the United Church of Canada, authorized by the General Synod and the General Council, 1971, hymn 69. Perhaps the point we are seeking to make here can be helpfully illustrated by a statement Bonhoeffer makes in one of his letters from prison. He writes: "Speaking frankly, to long for the transcendent when you are in your wife's arms is, to put it mildly, a lack of taste, and it is certainly not what God expects of us. We ought to find God and love him in the blessings he sends us. If he pleases to grant us some overwhelming earthly bliss, we ought not to try to be more religious than God himself." *Letters and Papers from Prison*, ed. by Eberhard Bethge, tr. by Reginald H. Fuller, London, S.C.M. Press, 1953, p. 86.

7   This seems to me a fair summary of the argument in Pierre Teilhard de Chardin, *The Future of Man*, tr. by Norman Denny, Fontana Religious Books, 1969.

8   Bernard Lonergan, *Insight: A Study of Human Understanding*, London, Longmans, Green and Company, revised, 1958, p. 729.

9   See Rev. 21: 1-4; 22: 1-5; II Pe. 3: 13.

10   Karl Barth, *op. cit.*, Volume II, Part 2, p. 94.

CHAPTER 2

BEING, MAN AND GOD

There are two views of the relation of Being to man and God that theological assertions made in our first chapter call into question. Firstly there are philosophical-theological understandings that identify Being with God. There may be nothing that distorts the biblical understanding of the nature of God and man more than this identification. Sooner or later it will manifest these consequences: (a) it will depersonalize God into a Power, Structure, or Depth of Being that can be thought of as personal only, if at all, through man's relation to it; (b) everything is thought to be real to the extent that it participates in Being and therefore God is the essential reality of all things; (c) for man this means that God is his essential being so that his actual being as man is constituted by some kind of estrangement from God; (d) salvation becomes thereby understood as the recovery by man of his lost infinity, the return to unqualified union, indeed to identity of being with the Absolute from which the fall into the differentiated form of being that was human existence had taken place. From this perspective God sooner or later, in one way or another, must be viewed as "the enemy" of the humanity of man. Man has no reality, not simply apart from God, but other than God, so that in the fulfilment of his being man finally must surrender everything that makes him human in distinction from God. It is most revealing that as a final consequence of the identification of Being and God in the philosophical theology of Paul Tillich, the supreme moment of the revelation of the New Being in Jesus who is the Christ occurs in the Cross, for the Cross means the ultimate surrender of everything that is Jesus (i.e., humanity) to the Christ that he is (i.e., manifestation of God).[1] If we understand this position aright it means that to be supreme bearer of revelation and salvation requires finally the surrender of the humanity of the God-man. Something similar, though by no means identical, seems to be asserted also in this quotation from Karl Rahner:

> "The incarnation of God is ... the unique, supreme case of the total actualization of human reality, which consists of the fact that man *is* insofar as he gives himself up."[2]

Rahner's position does differ basically from that of Tillich. It represents the second view that we are constrained to call into question. For Rahner God is not identified with Being and therefore finite existence is not essentially estrangement from God. However, for him, the finite as finite is capable of Infinity and has Infinity as its End.[3] That is, man is made to be filled with the Being of God. This is precisely so of Jesus who in this regard as in others is the manifestation of true humanity and the destiny of every man. Jesus, as Jesus, is said to be "the finitude of the infinite Word of God himself", the one who actualizes the "potentia oboedientialis", "the possibility of human nature being assumed by the person of the Word of God".[4]

We will return to Rahner later but let us stay a little longer with what we understand to be other consequences of the identity of God with being as we find it in Paul Tillich. What is true supremely of man, must also be true of every kind of creaturely reality. Whatever reality it has comes from its participation in Being, i.e., God. It is a *finite* form of being because as finite it participates in non-being as well.[5] This means that nothing finite, including man, can be worthful in itself, can have meaning or significance in its creaturely nature as such. It derives significance only from the degree of power, or form, or mystery of Being in which it participates and which it may manifest. All things are real to the extent that they point beyond themselves to God. Such an understanding would seem to imply that the individual as individual cannot be loved simply for itself but also always and mainly for the Other-than-itself that it expresses. This we have called a religious, sacramental view of the so-called created order. Its ultimate consequences I think is the loss of love for all save God. God is the reality that is sought in all things. God is not the name for the free Word and Spirit that first of all creates the creature as an object of love and then, if the creature be human, sets him free for the love of other creatures God has made. Rather God is the name of the Reality to be sought in all things, even in human personal reality such as neighbour and self. In the identification of Being and God, both God and man as realities to whom the scriptures bear witness become lost. God no longer in any strictly meaningful sense can be thought of as that Being who, having given being to an altogether other than himself comes to identify himself with that other in its death that it as such might live. God cannot be seen to be the one who being rich in God-ness became the poor of the other-than-himself in its estranged and dying estate, in order that by that poverty he might restore to the loved one the riches of a creature's life. Rather it is the contrary that would seem to be asserted here. It is through the poverty of the creature, the self-surrender of everything that is Jesus unto death, that Being as such is enriched, that New Being is made manifest. The humanity of man is lost in the manifestation of the reality of God. Human being as such has no self-fulfilling destiny.

We have already noted in our reference to Rahner another view of God in his relation to man, and the world, that our theological understanding developed in the first chapter also calls into question. It is a view that seems to be more faithful to a biblical understanding of creation, and of the reality of creaturely being that is distinct from the Being of God. Yet, because of its basic orientation, it also proves inimical to the genuine humanity of man. There do appear at times in Rahner also expressions that seem to go in the direction of the identification of God with Being. We have in mind in particular his work *Spirit in the World*.[6] In the introduction to it a contributor writes: "He (i.e., Rahner) proposes a transcendental understanding of God, who is not known by man as an object of reality, but as principle of human knowledge and reality." But basically and on the whole in Rahner's theology a distinction is clearly made between finite and infinite being, that is between the being that is appropriate to man, and all other creatures, and the Being of God. God is the supreme Being who gives power to be to the other-than-himself. Therefore created being, not essentially estranged from God, is able to have a limited, derived, yet nonetheless real significance and meaning in itself. But the arrow of faith being turned in the direction of transcendence, from the creature to the Creator, from time to eternity, from earth to heaven, this relative meaning and significance in the end are also lost in God. For from this perspective too the true, essential, *all-absorbing* meaning of creaturely reality is its orientation to God. Man's openness towards God, his freedom for God, his capacity for receiving God, his destiny to be filled as finite being with the infinity of God, constitute the reality of his being as man. In accordance with God's intention for man, he begins as a natural creature participating in a natural life. But his vocation and his destiny are to become supernaturalized, "deified", by his reception of the Being of God. Representing a kindred view, the Anglican theologian, E. Mascall, writes: "In the natural order we live the finite life of a creature, while in the supernatural order we live the infinite life of God, even while we who live it are finite creatures and can therefore live it only in our finite way."[7] Mascall quotes with approval the statement of Emile Mersch:

> "The infinite Being has two ways of giving himself to finite beings; by the former he gives himself to them in *their* way, which makes them themselves; by the latter, he give himself to them in *his* way, which makes them one with him."[8]

Mascall further quotes with approval Augustine: "God wishes to make you a god, not by nature but by adoption. Thus the whole man is deified."[9]

There is a great deal in the theology of Karl Rahner that goes in this direction. Indeed for him the destiny of deification determines much of man's life in the natural order itself.

> "Every venture into the world shows itself to be borne by the ultimate desire of the spirit for absolute being; every entrance into sensibility, into the world and its destiny, shows itself to be only the coming to be of a spirit which is striving towards the absolute."[10]

At certain points in his theological reflection Rahner shows a sensitivity for the implication of this understanding of human nature and destiny for the humanity of man. At times he seems to pull back from these consequences in the name, one supposes, of love for the humanity of man. On the one hand he says, reminding us of Tillich, "Man is pure reference to God. He ... is a mystery always referred beyond himself into the mystery of God."[11] But shortly afterwards he comes to say:

> "The true God is not the one who kills that he himself can live. He is not 'the truly real' which like a vampire draws to himself and so to speak sucks out the proper reality of things different from himself; He is not the *esse omnium*. The nearer one comes to him, the more real one becomes; the more he grows in and before one, the more independent one becomes oneself."[12]

What is said here is very true! But can it be sustained without contradiction in a theology that sees man's destiny as deification, one wherein man's finitude is finally to be filled with the infinity of God? It is true that for Rahner, unlike Tillich, since God is not the *esse omnium*, man need not die that God might fully live. But if man's very being is so constituted that it is by nature only oriented toward transcendence, toward the absolute, if man is made "to be endowed with the radical infinity of the absolute God",[13] is not the end result that his humanity is swallowed up by deity; is man not regarded simply as the human stage whereon God plays out his human life? We too shall have to affirm with eager, joyous acceptance that there is in man's relation to God a determination of his being by God. But such a relationship is not in itself the sum of man's being as man. Rather as heart of man's being it is the fountain source of a freedom, willed by God, that is even in a sense freedom from God, the expression of a will on God's part that man be free for himself, his neighbour and the world. Man's destiny is not to be filled with the infinity of God but to be enabled by God's infinite grace to achieve a genuine human existence, finite and free.

If the freedom of man is thought to be only freedom in God for God, if the fulfilment of his nature as man is to be found in the fact that, as Schillebeeckx says, "he goes out of himself toward God",[14] if all his dealings with the world, presumably including those with fellow-man, are to be thought of only as "a moment in our dialogue with God"[15] what, to quote the phrase of Rahner, "proper reality of things different from (God)" in any significant sense remains? In what sense can it be affirmed that the nearer one comes to God ... "the more independent one becomes oneself"? Surely this religious understanding of man's nature and destiny sets its religious stamp on the totality of man's life in time, insofar as man here and now must live in accordance with the eternal goal toward which he moves and strives. Hegel defined religion as "the self-elevation of man ... from finite life to infinite life".[16] The theologians we have cited would not wish to speak of the transition from finite to infinite life in terms of the "self-elevation" of man. Nevertheless, for them too as with Hegel man has a super-human destiny. He is one who is destined to have his being solely determined by the Being of God who wills to live in him a divine life humanly.

In accord with theological understanding set out in our first chapter we must find error in every attempt to identify Being and God. Indeed we find it necessary to assert with Pascal, and against Tillich,[17] that the Being or God of philosophy and the God of Christian faith are quite different realities. A philosophical concept of being may be a useful, perhaps even intellectually necessary, construct of reason that serves to order and unify rationally our experience and understanding of the world. But the concept of Absolute Being, as a philosophical concept, is a "relative Absolute" — an absolute relativized for the Christian believer by the Reality of God who names himself as the Wholly Other not naturally available to man. Thus, we do not need to deny man's philosophical understanding of reality in the name of God. We simply contest its dominating self-sufficiency in view of the sovereign finality that is God in his self-revealing Word. On the basis of that revelation one must assert a distinction between two types of being — two *kinds*, not to speak of two *dimensions*, of reality. There is the reality of God, and the reality of all that is not he. God alone is self-being in the sense that his power of being lies solely in himself. Then there are other kinds of reality which depend for being on God. The being that they have is not God's being. It is creaturely being. It has its own kind of self-being but only from that power to be that God gives to it. It is creation, finite reality, being apart from God, with a power to be such given originally and constantly by God.

Above we avoided deliberately speaking of God as a dimension of reality taken as a whole. For God is not simply that transcendence that is our being's ground and goal. In our understanding of Christian truth, nature is not ordered (by nature or grace) to super-nature as constituent structure of its own being. Rather in the freedom of self-determining love, as a supreme act of grace, God orders himself toward nature in that loving expression of his will that creation is. Therefore creations's value, so to speak, does not lie solely in the fact that God decides to love and accept it. Nor does it lie in the sacramental character of its capacity to point to God. God made it to be good in a finite, creaturely kind of goodness that inheres itself. The meaning and significance of creaturely existence does not reside in the fact that it provides a pathway to God. There is no pathway to God through nature and that's not what nature's for! It is true that in the biblical witness to the Creator and creation, nature is said to join in a paean of praise to the Creator, as creaturely being glorifying God and giving expression to the wonder of his love. The psalmist calls on nature generally to join with man in offering such hymns of praise to God. But the God who is thus praised is he who is disclosed not through nature but through the uniqueness of the community's history and in that history he is disclosed as the God who seeks the creature's good. When nature in man becomes de-natured, refusing to be simply nature and aspiring to be like God, God acts in a yet more wondrous exercise of grace to set it free from its bondage to evil and evil's consequence that in the power of his gifts of reconciliation and redemption it might find the power to be itself again.

So God preserves nature from becoming de-natured by the use of it generally as a stepping-stone to him. Since the man of faith finds God to be self-revealed in a particular history of revelation — wherein nature and history do indeed have sacramental meaning and purpose — he finds that all other times and places, all other persons and things, may have a secular meaning and intent. Not all bushes are intended to be burning bushes, not all human speaking is intended to be prophecy, not all history is intended in itself to be salvation history, not every thought and action of man is intended to be directed toward God. In saying so we are not, I hope and believe, guilty of rebellious attitudes. To the contrary, we find here an occasion to glorify God in the wonder of his self-giving love, even as we seek to speak truly of his intention for the man he has made.

Of course, if in his human history man does not begin with God, if he is fighting God, or fleeing from him in the world — if he is sinner, not justified by grace through faith, and not sanctified by positive response to God's Spirit working in him — then the claim of God upon him must be an all-demanding, all-absorbing claim. If he does not — will not — seek God's kingdom first, then he is not free to enjoy and fulfil nature, including his own. Being himself idolatrous, he will make idols of all else besides. Creaturely reality will take on some kind of meaning of God for him. But we are speaking here of God's original, unrevoked, enduring intent — and sin and evil had no place in God's original intention for creation. God willed that man, walking by faith in him and holding converse with him in the times that are right for worship, should find other times for holding converse too with nature and fellow-man, set free by God from God (so to speak) for the world. Allowing God to be God, self-named in a specific revelation, self-given in particular ways, at particular times and places, allows nature to be at other times and places simply nature and not a sacramental place to look for God. Room is thus provided, by God's own intent, for the love of persons and things in their radical uniqueness and particularity. They may be loved for themselves and not simply as symbols of some transcendent reality toward which they serve to point. Of course all persons and things do participate in and express creaturely powers of being in general even as each person and thing expresses them in its own peculiar way. But our point is that it is as such that they may be known and loved. The quest need no longer be (for it was not, is not by God intended to be) a search for God in finite persons and things. We may, like Chesterton, enjoy the universal in the particular, the inkyness of ink, and the wetness of water. But in such enjoyment in the goodness of creation we need not, should not, seek the Creator of all. So it can also be that with all living beings, and most surely with persons, it is the particular and not the universal that is especially remarked and loved. When God is allowed to be God, and nature nature, the universal is no more significant than the particular. God is no nearer, so to speak, to the general than he is to the unique. Indeed, does not Jesus witness in the Gospel that not one sparrow falls but that the Father sees it and that each hair on each person's head is numbered by him whose love is greater than a universal love for mankind?

So God is not the end, the meaning and purpose, sought in every relation we have with the world. He is the one we start from, the one through whom and with whom we approach the world. We love the world in and with God's love for the world. We do not seek him in all things. We seek all things through him. He is not the horizon in the sense of being the goal of all our looking. He wills to be the "first found" in whom and with whom all else is given.[18] At once centre and circumference of our being and life, he wills to set us free for the world he loves, with a power for loving that derives from him. We are pleased to find in Rahner a statement that can be understood in such a way as to sum up many of the points we are wishing to make here:

"Leaving creatures is the first and, for us sinners, always new phase of finding God. Yet it is merely the first stage. Service towards creatures, the mission away from God back into the world, may be the second phase. Yet there is still a third: to find the very creature itself, in its independence and autonomy, *in* God, in the midst of the jealously burning inexorableness of His being all-in-all, to find the creature even in the very midst of this — the small in the great, the circumscribed in the boundless, the creature (the very creature itself) in the Creator — this is only the third and highest phase of our relationship with God."[19]

We said earlier in passing that if man does not begin with God made manifest in a special revelation he is bound to go looking for him in nature and human history generally. This universal quest of man for God is undoubtedly the presupposition of the words Simeon speaks in W. H. Auden's *Christmas Oratorio* "For the Time Being":

"Because of his visitation, we may no longer desire God as if He were lacking: our redemption is no longer a question of pursuit but of surrender to Him who is always and everywhere present."[20]

The question to which our discussion now leads is whether or not there is inevitably in every human heart a passion for the infinite and whether the God of revelation is necessarily the object of that desire. I am no longer certain that it is so — that if any particular individual will not find God in the

15

history of his self-revelation that culminates in Jesus, he is bound to go on a religious quest for God elsewhere. That is, though I believe every man has by nature so-called religious capacities, it does not inevitably mean that he is always engaged in a religious quest. Many today do not seem to be restless souls expressing infinite desire for God, or experiencing profound emptiness of soul because he has not yet been found. It could be that our scientific age has produced "one dimensional" men[21] who show little if any passion for the infinite. On the other hand, I cannot escape the conviction that there is in the human spirit an indestructible capacity for transcendence that at any time may be, and always in due time, in human history will be, awakened. But our point is that the God of revelation is not the object of man's capacity for transcendence any more than God is the name for the transcendent reality man may find. It is not the arrow of faith that flies in the direction of transcendence but man's natural spirit with its capacity to know creation's depth or height. However, God does indeed, through His spirit, create hunger in the human heart for himself. "As the hart panteth after the water-brook, so longs my soul after Thee, O God." (Psalm 42:1) Jesus calls them blessed who hunger after God in his righteousness and promises that they will be filled. (S. Mtt. 6:6) But this hunger of which the Bible speaks always has in mind, I believe, God's Word and does not express a general longing of the spirit for the Absolute.

If a person or community is "without God in the world" then both hungers of the human spirit, that which God induces for his Word and that which nature calls forth with her mystery, will find expression in idolatry. Man will inevitably succumb to the temptation to make idols for himself as substitute for God and engage in various attempts at self-redemption. The "religious life" of man without God is always such. And in it not only God but the creature too loses its integrity. Forced to serve as surrogate for God, it is forced to become a means to an end it can never realize. It loses its natural beauty, wonder, usefulness. No wonder nature is said by the apostle to be in bondage waiting for man's redemption. Rahner in the quotation cited above stated that in order to find God truly, the creature and love for the creature which stands in the place of God has to be surrendered. "Leaving creatures is the first and, for us sinners, always new phase of finding God." The idolatrous attachment of sinful man to created things has to be broken in a spiritual act of conversion that is a virtual forsaking of the world. This Soren Kierkegaard knew and Gerard Manley Hopkins, as did also August-ine and before these the Apostle Paul. Yet all these persons also bear witness that, in a miracle of grace, the surrendered world is given back again to those who seek God and his kingdom first. Only when God is allowed to be God, is the creature preserved as creature in all its marvellous, mysterious, lovely creaturehood. And, when God is faithfully, lovingly permitted to be God in accord with his self-declared Being and Will, he will — as he did "in the beginning" with Adam — turn man toward the creature as subject suited for his love.   Not to love God in the creature, but to love the creature in God is the will of God for man.

It is not, therefore, altogether wrong to say that man without God is an empty soul and that such emptiness may lead man to seek in the creature a fulfilment no creature can provide.   But it is wrong, I think, to speak as Rahner does generally of man as a mystery of *infinite* emptiness, and to speak of God as that mystery which fills man with his own infinite fulness.   This is how Rahner puts it in his own words: God is "the One who has decided to fill this infinite emptiness (which is the mystery of man) with his own infinite fullness (which is the myster of God)."[22]   This is but another way of speaking about God as man's lost, or not yet acquired infinity.   Its consequence in the end is the loss of humanness.

Man has indeed lost God in the world.   He needs not so much to find him, as power, form, abyss of being — a lost infinity or a future infinity toward which a process of deification tends — but rather to be found of him who in the beginning found it good to grant him creaturehood, a capacity for being human in the world; and who mysteriously and wonderfully found it still better to restore to him his lost humanity in Jesus Christ.   In Jesus Christ God gives himself and creates our new humanity.   Neither deified man, nor homonized Creator, he is at once truly God and truly man, come that we — forgiven — might once more have God at the heart of life and therein find our freedom to be human in the world.

FOOTNOTES

1   See Paul Tillich, *Systematic Theology*, Volume II, Chicago University Press, 1957, p. 123.

2   Karl Rahner, *Theological Investigations*, Volume IV, London, Darton, Longman and Todd, Baltimore, Helicon Press, 1966, p. 110.

3   Karl Rahner, *op. cit.*, Volume V, 1966, p. 10.   "Listen to Christianity as the message which does not forbid anything except man's shutting-himself-off in his finite nature, except man's refusal to believe that he is endowed with the radical infinity of the absolute God and that the *finitum* is *capax infiniti.*"

4   Karl Rahner, *op. cit.*, Volume IV, p. 110.

5   See Paul Tillich, *op. cit.*, Volume I, p. 189.

6   Karl Rahner, *Spirit in the World*, tr. by William Dych, New York, Herder & Herder, 1968, pp. xliii-xliv.

7   E. L. Mascall, *The Importance of Being Human:* Some Aspects of the Christian Doctrine of Man, New York, Columbia University Press, 1958, p. 66.

8   *Ibid*, pp. 65-66

9   *Ibid*, pp. 63-64.

10   Karl Rahner, *op. cit.*, p. 407.

11   Karl Rahner, *Theological Investigations*, Volume III, p. 31.

12   *Ibid*, p. 40.

13   Karl Rahner, *op. cit.*, Volume V, p. 10.

14   E. Schillebeeckx, *God and Man*, tr. by E. Fitzgerald and P. Tomlinson, New York, Sheed and Ward, 1969, p. 216.

15   *Ibid*, p. 224.

16   Quoted in Charles West, *The Power to be Human*, New York, Macmillan, 1971, pp. 106-107.

17   cf. Paul Tillich, *Bibilical Religion and the Search for Ultimate Reality*, University of Chicago Press, 1955, p. 85.

18   See S. Mtt. 6: 33; I Cor. 3: 22-23.

19   Karl Rahner, *op. cit.*, Volume III, 1967, p. 43.

20   W. H. Auden, "For the Time Being: A Christmas Oratorio" in *The Collected Poetry of W. H. Auden*, New York, Random House, 1945, p. 454.

21   The phrase is borrowed from Herbert Marcuse, *One Dimensional Man:* Studies in the ideology of advanced industrial society, Boston, Beacon Press, 1964.

22   Karl Rahner, *op. cit.*, Volume V, 1966, p. 8.

CHAPTER 3

WORSHIP AS SACRAMENTAL OCCASION

When the arrow of faith follows the flight of God's movement outward from himself toward the world, there is no sense in which this flight traces a movement of essential separation or estrangement from God. If we speak of a movement from God towards the world, into the world, we are not speaking of any kind of Neo-Platonic fall, any progressive decline in Being from the divine fulness toward spirit-increasingly-encumbered-by-matter, so that the history of creation becomes a history of further and further separation from God and the history of salvation a history of gradual ascent back toward lost union with him. Rather the movement outward from himself toward the world and into the world is a constant movement of God's love expressed in gracious deeds expressive of his will. God, as we have said, does not simply will himself; he wills the world and man as creature in the world and master of the world as child of God. Moreover, the movement outward from Self toward world, and man in the world, includes God's making himself known to man, and available to man, not that such knowledge is exhaustive of man's good, as religious views would have it, but that God might be the centre and circumference of man's life. There is a true and profound sense in which it is right to say that man has been made for God. It is witnessed in the commandment that expresses the gracious truth of his being as a child of God, "Thou shalt love the Lord thy God with all thyself." The love of the self for God is a condition of being human and free. Our self-conscious, responding relation to God who reveals himself as loving Lord is not something added to our nature as men. It is not a religious dimension of our being, so to speak — as though we could be human without it and super--human with it. Nor, contrarywise, is God a term used to speak of religious aspiration or a quality of human existence at its best. God is self-being, Wholly Other, existing in his own right. We are made for a relation with God thus understood, a relation that is dialogical, without which we are not truly human or humanly free. It is false service to man in quest for understanding and fulfilment of his humanity to tell him that theology rightly understood is anthropology, that God is the name for a process albeit with a transcendent aspect, through which humanity evolves and men are made. "There is", says Gregory Baum, "no human standpoint from which God faces man simply as a divine Thou ... God is present in my knowledge of the important truth, he can never be object of knowledge ... present in every act of true love, never the Invisible Lover facing me."[1] If Baum's intention here were simply to say that God in his self-disclosure to man uses finite instruments for purposes of revelation, that we encounter God supremely when his glory is seen in a (particular!) human face, we could have no difficulty agreeing with him. But the quotation, I think, has other meanings in mind. It takes us rather far in the opposite direction, of seeing God in every human face, in every truth that enlightens the mind. It seems to deny that there is a specific sense in which it is right to speak of man encountering God in special "I-Thou" ways. Something similar occurs in the writings of Teilhard de Chardin:

> "Christ gives himself to us through the world which is to be con-summated in relation to him. By means of all created things without exception, the divine assails us, penetrates us and moulds us. We imagined it as distant and inaccessible, whereas in fact we live steeped in its burning layers."[2]

On this passage Rubem Alvez comments while continuing the citation:

> "As we meet the cosmos we are really facing the 'universal Smile' which creates that 'taste for being', because through the world 'being ... became, in some way, tangible and savorous' to us."[3]

We have seen that the identification of God and being leads precisely in the direction in which these quotations would seem to have us go. There are it would seem in modern Christian thought more varied examples of self-transcending naturalism than Tillich's. But this road, we have affirmed, is not a right road to follow in quest of God, world and our true humanity. On it I believe we will find that sooner or later man's humanity is lost in the affirmation of God's being and/or God's deity is lost in its identification with some power of man. Always to lose God is to lose man, and a sure way of losing both is to identify both at any level of meaning and significance — apart of course from the radically unique one, Jesus Christ.

God is the Wholly Other, supreme personal will, who wills to be present for and with man as the subject of personal love. If the "I-Thou" form of personal address between God and man, and man and God, is lost from human consciousness, if for modern men the biblical witness, in language of this kind, has no longer power to grasp the hearer with a convincing sense of reality and truth (no matter what efforts must be expended interpreting their meaning) man will have lost not so much a dimension of human existence as the very centre and circumference of his life.

God is the *centre* of human existence in that to give oneself to him in a total personal act of love is the essential humanizing act of our being as men. God is the *circumference* of our existence in that this personal act of self-giving love does not absorb or exhaust all God-given capacities for being human in the world. Rather it is the creative source and ground for freedom to accomplish our humanity in subordinate ways. God is thus the "sur-round", the context for all our life, even as he is at the centre of every life that is truly human and free.   He is both he in whom we live and move and have our being, and he who confronts us in his personal Word of judgement and grace.

Now God, as sustaining origin of our being, centre and circumference of human life, is always present to and with us in the world, but present in differing ways.   As sustaining source of being God is hidden in his presence to the world.   It is as Creator that it is right to say that to know God as *absent*, i.e., as one not available to human capacities of knowing, is the right way of knowing his *presence*.[4]   As Creator he is present to the world, not in it.   But he who is thus present in his absence becomes present with and for us in the utterance of his Word.   He who is essentially hidden acts in special ways to make himself known.   That his self-revealing action has taken the form of redemptive history is due to the fact that from the beginning, i.e., since man was man, God was lost from the centre of human life.   But the lost God willed to be found by finding them who having lost him had lost themselves in the world.   Through redemptive deed and inspired witness he sought in forgiving love to make himself once more available to men that we might not ever be without God in the world and thus ever without power to effect our true humanity.

Now our effort at the moment cannot be to rehearse the gospel of the self-revealing God.   Our purpose is rather to show something of the significance and import of the theme for our understanding of God's intention for man in the world.   In this chapter we wish in particular to explore that intention with respect to worship, to ask about the role of worship in a perspective of faith that acknowledges in God what might be called a worldly intent.   A major point to be made here is the simple and well-known one that at the heart of God's love for us is his will to commune with men. And communion implies Otherness — an over-againstness that transcends all barriers and overcomes all resistance and enters into a fellowship of love.   On commenting on *Hesed*-love in Hosea and Jeremiah, Eichrodt says:

> "The marvellous quality of this love is seen to reside not only
> in the condescension of the exalted God but also much more
> inwardly in the mystery of the divine will which seeks commun-
> ion with man."[5]

God wills to enter into loving fellowship with man, in a relationship that cannot rightly be spoken of save in the language of "I and Thou".

Now the locus of this bid for communion on the part of God is not heaven but earth, accomplished not in heavenly but in earthly ways.   God does not encounter man in that fellowship of love that is central to man's existence in some inner, mysterious depth of human spirituality.   Indeed, the word "encounter" itself is meant to state that the event of which we are speaking is not some kind of mystical union of the self with its transcendent source.

There are, as we said before and will repeat later, experiences of creation's mysterious depth or height for which "heaven" stands as symbol — the heaven that God has made. There may indeed be wonderful, mysterious, mystical experiences for which some eminent men of genius have capacity, which belong to the filled-out human life of which God is the circumference. Human culture yields and must find room for man's creative accounts of his experience of this dimension of his world. But to confuse these "religious" experiences with experiences of God, or to confuse men's inspired account of them with God's Word, is to fall prey to that idolatry that confuses the creature with the Creator and leads to the loss of the mystery, and the wonder appropriate to both. The religious genius, like the artistic genius with whom he has much in common, serves to open up to our vision and perhaps experiment, dimensions of existence closed until disclosed to more pedestrian spirits. But it is of the gods they speak, not of God! For God is truly spoken of only through the servants he chooses to be witnesses of his Word given through special, radically unique moments of self-revelation in nature and human history. Not mystical, religious experience but *faith* is the correlate of revelation. "Faith", says the apostle, "comes from what is heard, but what is heard comes from the preaching of Christ." (Ro. 10:17).

We have said that there surely is a sense in which it is true to say God has made man for himself. We understand this to mean at least two things: (a) that communion with God is God's will and man's supreme good; (b) that the total self-commitment in love of man to God is both essential to true human existence and ground for the freedom that enables man to actualize all human powers in self-fulfilling ways. In the biblical story of creation witness is made to the fact that God willed to walk with man in the garden of the world, a hidden but unimagineably near one, giving man being, setting him free for his humanity, as husband and wife, as husbandman of the world, providentially serving man in protecting him from evil, guiding his feet into the ways of truth. But from time to time God calls man into personal fellowship with himself, addressing to him a personal word of love and truth, seeking from man a response of acknowledgement and praise and above all a totally trusting act of self-realizing love. What continuing form this personal word of divine address and human response would have taken had man not fallen, in those times of worship which we have defined as God meeting with man in the dialogic relation of "I and Thou", we do not know. We do know that in actuality that word of self-communicating love has taken the form and content of the gospel of Jesus Christ. Through pride man refused the vocation to give himself to God in loving trust and trusting love and thereby lost his freedom to fill out his human life within the world in creative, non-destructive ways. To save man from the loss of both the centre and the sum of his humanity, God acted in a redemptive history that culminates in Jesus and that history has become for us the meaning of God's Word. All worship is in essence the service of that Word.

Worship is the moment in human existence when in response to God's calling we allow him to be the focal centre of our consciousness, of our attention. It is the sacramental moment when everything — every thought, every word, every action is intended to be bearer, servant, mediator of his reality and truth. It is the moment when God wills to be present and available to man in disclosed rather than hidden ways. Here indeed all human language is rightly language about God. There are, we have asserted, other times in human existence, when creaturely realities, fellow man, nature, the exercise and results of human creativity, rightfully and not sinfully occupy the focal point of human interest. The God who gave men and women one to another as suitable mates and who called man to name the animals and perform other acts of humanizing the world is not jealous of those moments when in consciousness he does not occupy centre-stage. For God, as we have said, willed and made possible creaturely dimensions of goodness that do not derive their goodness from the immediacy of their bearing upon him. To each its time and place; and to each its order in the sequence of times and places. There is a time and place for worship; and in the sequence of times and places in relation to its significance for life, worship is supreme. Then, indeed, God wills to occupy centre-stage. Then God does will that all language, verbal and enacted, shall have reference to him, weighted with symbolic meaning and significance as vehicle of witness to him. Worship is sacramental through and through, to the end of bringing God and man into communion, in the address of God to man of his judging, forgiving, renewing, liberating Word of love.

Now such worship does not intend or serve the filling up of man's finitude with the infinity of God; nor does it serve to allow man to partake in some mystical fashion of the eternal conversation of God with God. Man has neither as his nature nor his destiny to become a kind of fourth person in the Trinity, if I may say so reverently and I hope not mistakenly. Rather, while telling man who he is in acts of revelation which on reflection yield the doctrine of God's triunity, worship is for the purpose of allowing God to tell man of his love for him and of allowing man to respond in words and deeds of answering love. To know *humanly* God as he is in himself is to know Reality. To act in accord with that knowledge is to avoid idolatry. The worship of God thus known has at its heart God's word of fogiving, renewing, promising love in Jesus Christ spelled out in terms of God's gracious intent for man including the abundance of a finite life fulfilled within the limits of its finitude. The worship we have mainly in mind here is the public worship of God. Believing witness to the gospel when accompanied by God's presence in the Spirit, creates a community of faith and love which engages in worship as central to its life.

In public worship the believing community not only celebrates its having had its origins in God but seeks to be reconstituted anew by its Creator and Lord. The Church owes its being to the believing reception of God's self-

23

giving in Jesus Christ and divine Spirit.   Having this origin, it is called Body of Christ and Spiritual Community.   As Jesus promised Peter the Christian Church is founded upon the believing reception of the faithful witness to him as the Christ, Son of the living God. (S. Mtt. 16:13-18) This good news being heard and received in faith, a community is created which is essentially indestructible.   The meaning of "infallibility" as understood by the Roman Catholic Hans Küng is one that can be readily accepted by the Protestant community, namely that the gospel when believingly proclaimed and received, creates a community that is indefectible.[6]   This does not mean that the Church is incapable of error against truth in its doctrinal expression, or against love in its actual life.   But is does mean that the Church will not depart so far from the reality and truth of the gospel as to be completely overpowered by unbelief.   Therefore the Church will always seek occasions to celebrate the gospel as the original and continuing source of its life.

We have spoken of the gospel as God's giving of himself in incarnate Word and empowering Spirit.   The public celebration of the gospel is therefore not adequately understood simply as an occasion for the Church to inform herself of the "truths of faith" that are important to her life, or the ethics of Christian behaviour that are implied in her belief.   These are essential aspects of the total life of the believing community.   They have their place in worship too.   But the public celebration of God should be conceived primarily as an occasion for divine — human encounter, when through a ministry appropriate to it, the living God comes to give himself to men.   Such a ministry is the ministry of Word and Sacrament.

By the ministry of Word within the context of public celebration is meant the sermon.   The sermon is not primarily conceived of as instruction in the truths of faith or the moral implicates of sound believing, though such elements will not be lacking from it.   The sermon is primarily conceived of as a service whereby the living God may communicate with men, may give himself to them as Truth and Life.   God's Word (proclamation) is therefore "sacramental".   One who preaches intends so to witness to the reality and truth of God as self-revealed that his human words become earthly means of God's own self-giving.   The "dialogue sermon" that aims primarily at edification should not be thought of as fitting substitute for proclamation which intends divine self-communication.   In every sermon there should be an implicit "now hear this" as offer of good news matching the explicit "this is my body — take and eat" of the enacted Word we call the Sacrament. There are those who would maintain that the full diet of public worship would contain both forms of God's self-giving — through speech and action.

Need we add that basic to this self-giving of God through sermon and sacrament is his presence and action in the Holy Spirit? The recognition of this fact through the invocation of God's presence in his Spirit is an essential mark of every act of public celebration.

"How", asked the apostle, "are men to call upon him in whom they have not believed?   And how are they to believe in him whom they have never heard?   And how are they to hear without a preacher?   And how can men preach unless they are sent?" (Romans 10: 14-15).

It may seem that this text has more to do with the missionary situation of the early Christian community than with its established practice of public worship.   But there is a certain sense in which the Church is always in a missionary situation and this fact determines some of the essential aspects of its public celebration.   We have already noted the role of proclamation in the constitution of the Church as community of faith and love.   The human word of witness to the living God aims at the conversion of both those who have never believed and those who never perfectly believe.   Faith, not being a possession, but always a gift, must constantly be renewed.   So the announcement of the evangel is always for the evangelistic purpose of conquering unbelief.   Yet, since the community that meets for worship is a believing one and many in the congregation are through baptism and confirmation dedicated to the life in faith, proclamation also serves the purposes of strengthening and edification.   The intention to grow in faith and love is not irrelevant to the public celebration of God, though, for reasons already given, such intention must find expression in activities that flow out from and carry beyond the worship of God.   Here the concept of celebration is a help in understanding the purpose of public worship.   The event of worship where "meeting" takes place, is more akin to a "happening" in personal encounter than an occasion for reflection on the implicates of faith and love.

Beyond these few simple affirmations of the Church's worship we cannot now go.   Our purpose has been simply to state that in accord with God's will for human life there are sacramental occasions, and that there is in fact a community in which we are called by him to lead a sacramental life.   Some perhaps might think it more consistent with our initial theme about the arrow of faith leading into the world, to assert that all human existence in the here and now is, so to speak, sacramental; that every meal man eats with fellowman in an attitude of accepting love, is a Lord's Supper, eaten and drunk in the presence of Jesus.   Such views I think are not true.   They tend on the one hand to lose the holiness of genuinely sacramental moments when God in his Word mediated through preaching and sacraments, addresses to men the word of their true and everlasting life.   On the other hand they also lose the genuine humanness of our encounter with one another on occasions of eating and drinking when we rejoice in the goodness of finite, creaturely life together, in the midst of which of course there is nothing to prevent us from uttering a cry of thanks to God, our Creator, for the goodness of creation and the freedom he gives for a joyful, filled-out human life.   The sacramental occasions, when the devout concentration on God who offers himself in his Son incarnate and Holy Spirit, are the times for allowing God to be God at the centre of our life as men, and for knowing that communion with God which is our supreme good. They are also occasions through which, freed from the guilt of our bondage to sins of idolatry and self-indulgence, and renewed through Word and Spirit in the image of God's earthly Son, we are set free for the abundant life of man with fellow-man and nature, for which the Son promised to set us free. Such worship also is the bulwark against the dire consequence of the confusion of kinds of reality one with the other that we encountered when we discussed the relation of Being and God. For all significant occasions in human life to be interpreted as sacramental occasions is to lose not only the profound significance for human life of the alternation of differing times and places. It is to lose at once much of the wonder and mystery of the glory of God and the wonder and mystery of finite reality as well. God out of justice toward himself and out of love for the creatures of his creating does not will either to happen.

FOOTNOTES

1   Gregory Baum in *The Ecumenist*, Volume IX, No. 1-2, p. 17.

2   Quoted in Rubem Alves, *A Theology of Human Hope*, Washington/Cleveland, Corpus Books, 1969, p. 150.

3   *Ibid.*

4   cf. some very significant things that are said about the "presence" and "absence" of God in Kornelis H. Miskotte, *When the gods are silent*, tr. by J. W. Doberstein, Harper and Row, 1967.

5   Walter Eichrodt, *Theology of the Old Testament*, Volume I, tr. by J. A. Baker, Philadelphia, Westminster Press, 1961, pp. 238-239.

6   See Hans Küng, *The Church* , tr. by R. and R. Ockenden, New York, Sheed & Ward, 1967, p. 342.

CHAPTER 4

SERVICE

In the worship of the Church reference is often made to the freedom man finds in the service of God. Many will know the prayer:

"O Thou who are the Light of the minds that know Thee, the Life of the souls that love Thee, and the Strength of the wills that serve Thee; help us so to know Thee that we may truly love Thee, so to love Thee that we may fully serve Thee, whom to serve is perfect freedom; ..."[1]

I wish to explore with you now the question of what service is in which the spirit finds its freedom in God, and a further question whether that freedom of the human spirit is intended by God to find expression also in play. What is the nature of service that distinguishes it from play? And what is the dialectic between service and play that enables man to fulfil the freedom of spirit in ways that are willed by God?

By service we mean all the actions of man that arise out of man's determination by God. In imitation of the Servant, Jesus Christ, we in our own manner of service seek to "work the works of God." Service is the corresponding activity of man to the working of God in and through him. By play we mean the self-determining action of man, wherein, set free by God "from God", man is not agent but master of what is said and done. In play man determines his own purposes and intent.

Is there any room in Christian thought and life for such a conception of play? Has God willed to be the *sole* determiner of all that man is and does? Has he willed in nature and human history to be alone the master of what takes place, so that every expression of freedom that is not freedom in service must be seen as evil or sin? Does man's actual exercise of human powers for free self-determination, in no matter what sphere of human accomplishment, bear the stamp of sin — that is as seen from the perspective of God? To be more specific, is human culture understood as the creation of the self-expression of the human spirit a sign *as such* of man's revolt from God? If I understand aright Jacques Ellul's book "The Meaning of the City"[2] his answer to the last question, and by implication to the others also, is "yes", God it would seem willed and still wills the exercise of human freedom *solely* in the function of service. Man sins precisely to the extent that he does not allow God to be in every particular the initiator and therefore the determiner of what he says and does. He builds his cities, creates culture and civilization through the exercise of human powers that are not fully determined by God.   For Ellul this is wrong *in principle!*   Man's rebellion expresses itself in the fact that his humanity is not exhaustively seen as locus and instrument of the divine action in and through him.   Man uses his freedom in self-determining ways and thereby manifests revolt.   God, in the forgiving love made manifest in Jesus, may indeed accept the results of human labour and creativity that we name culture, even as he accepts man the sinner into unwarranted fellowship with himself.   But these works of man's hands are not thought to be a fulfilment of God's original and abiding intention for man.   Nor are they achieved in the freedom for being human in the world that Jesus gives.   "Jesus", says Ellul, expressing what may be a literal truth but, I believe, falsely interpreted, "never proclaims grace for man's work."[3]   For God, presumably, never intended man to work in any sense in independence of him.

There are two quotations from Karl Barth that may seem at least by implication also to answer negatively the question about a distinction in man's use of freedom in service and play.   The first is as follows: "The ministry of witness forms the meaning and the scope of the whole of the Christian life."[4] The second is: "Service is the characteristic feature of the Christian life ... service can surely consist only in orienting and adapting one's human action to that of God, of the Lord."[5]   Barth here defines precisely and accurately what *service* is.   But does he mean to say that it and it alone exhausts God's intention for man?   "The ministry of witness forms the meaning and the scope of the whole of the Christian life."   There is a sense in which that is undoubtedly true.   But in what precise sense?   And in particular what in relation to the quotation about service?   Does it mean, for instance, that for the Christian all art and literature, all painting and poetry, every conversation that man has with fellow-man, every activity engaged in, should have as its immediate and direct intention to bear witness to God?   Is religion for Barth too, as it was for Tillich, the substance of culture — as culture is the form of religion?[6]   Surely not!   For we must remember Mozart!   Mozart whose genius lay for Barth in the fact that he knew what it was to *play!*[7]   Mozart who had creation not God as the subject matter of his creative expression.[8] Mozart, who (according to Barth's playful imagination) even in heaven, while Bach led the angels in hymns of praise to God — a most worthy service! — was engaged in the corner at play.   And God, Barth thought, was well-pleased with him.[9]   If it were not exceedingly presumptuous I would confess that one of the hopes I have for this series of lectures is that they might provide, in a theological statement that owes Barth a tremendous debt, and is often oriented in directions he indicates, a more consistent and secure place for Mozart than Barth's own theology as it stands seems to provide.

We do indeed believe that within a life of service that orients and adapts its human action to God the Lord, there is by God's intention a place for play, that is for an expression of the human spirit whereby man gives his own self-determined account of the meaning of being for him.   But play finds its true place only within a context of service, and derives freedom for play from the freedom that service provides. Therefore for this and other reasons of priority we must first deal with the question of what service is.

We have defined service as that activity of the human spirit that is and wills to be simply and solely determined by the action of God. There are two forms of such service one of which is universal and all-encompassing, the other more particular in kind. We speak first of the prime instance of the universal form of service.

There can be no doubt that God is the sole determiner of that activity of the human spirit whereby he becomes the centre and the circumference of human life. In creation God determined the being of man as one made for God at the centre of his life. Man was not simply made for a life that includes believing trust and responding love to God, as though these activities of his spirit might be regarded as the crowning achievement of an otherwise human life; man as made in God's image becomes human precisely through such activities as these. And when man through sin lost his humanity, that is lost the power to determine his life in accord with his nature as determined by God, God came to man in man as Jesus, to offer man forgiveness and restore in him once more the power to be man-for-God. In the life of Jesus, expressed in its totality as a life of trusting love and loving service, as the life of a servant who lived as he prayed, "not my will, but thine alone be done", we see the true life God intended for every man.

God makes this self-gift in Jesus, which is forgiveness and new life, available to us in the word of believing witness to it that he enables through his spirit. Through witness to the gospel he calls all men to himself to receive forgiveness and the new life of freedom in the service of love. This is the meaning now of having God at the centre and the circumference of human life — to hear and heed, in the Spirit, the gospel concerning God's son. To be Christian means to glorify God in a life of unqualified trust and unqualified love, with Jesus as its source and inspiration. Trust and love, thanksgiving and praise, mark the Christian life in all its aspects, individual and corporate. God is both the object of these and their all-determining source, power, meaning and end. Nothing that man is or does can fall outside the context, the will, the enablement of God's sovereign determination of our being with its freedom here. God in Jesus Christ has become the servant of man, that we might become the free servants of God, responding to God's determination of us in trusting love and grateful praise. If witness means to have life marked at its centre by such faithful and thoughtful commitment, certainly witness is the vocation of every man. Barth's word concerning it is true: "The ministry of witness forms the meaning and the scope of the whole of Christian life", though there may be reason to ask, before we are finished, whether a more comprehensive rubric for the Christian life, may be "gratitude", which may leave fuller scope for things that also belong to God's intention for man.

In a determination of human existence by God's Word and Spirit the Christian man and the Christian community are called by the gospel to a vast variety of expressions of faith and love in the performance of which the spirit of man is made truly free. Within the general calling to this kind of Christian life in freedom there are also specific callings, an analysis of which may help us to understand the difference we find between service and play.

There can be no doubt that just as God is the sole determiner of his Word, he is also the sole determiner of those who serve his Word. He alone controls the human history that is identical with his own divine Being, purpose and action — the history of Jesus. Solely by the grace of God that he, as Son of God was, did he become the obedient human servant of God in the salvation of men. In Jesus the man, the human work is and wills to be completely determined by the work of God in him. Jesus performs, and wills to perform, no other than the work of God. His life is lived solely as service and of it what Barth says is without remainder true: "Service can surely consist only in orienting and adapting one's human action to that of God the Lord."

And what is true of Jesus as human instrument of God's will and work in saving men has its counterpart in those called to the prophetic and apostolic witness of God's action in him.[10] They too in their service are or will to be determined solely by the action of God. They do not choose God but are chosen by him. They are called to perform their ministry solely in the service of the truth and the encouragement of love that God provides.

And so also is it with those who continue their service in the special form of ministry we call Word and Sacrament. This ministry is performed by those who believe themselves especially called to it. Here freedom for vocational choice is transcended through the firm conviction that one can do no other than respond to the call of God. There is allowed to men generally, even Christian men, freedom of choice concerning vocation, within the limits of what is morally acceptable and in accord with the norm of loving service of the neighbour and his good. But the vocation of ministry of Word and Sacrament is not an example of such vocations. The ministry of the Word is wrongly conceived as a creative exercise of human powers aimed primarily at making a contribution to human culture. There is, of course, in the performance of this ministry, abundant opportunity for the exercise of human powers, but solely under the control of the Word to which witness is made, and in the freedom that the Divine Spirit provides for such witnessing. To regard preaching, for instance, from the perspective of play, as an exercise of human gifts in using human language creatively, either as oratory or as literature, is to misunderstand the nature of preaching from the perspective of God's intent. Conversely, to regard the exercise of human gifts for using language creatively in the writing of poetry or prose, or in oration, or other modes of spoken communication, as service of the Word of God is to misunderstand human culture, also from the perspective of God's intent. Of course, just as the preacher wills to put at the service of God's Word all human powers and gifts, so it could be that in the free exercise of human gifts for creativity one may choose God and the things of God as subject matter of one's art. But the difference lies in the fact that in believing proclamation the servant gives himself over to the Word, the witness to which is the sole intent of his vocation, while in the case of the artist he himself determines the subject matter upon which he wills to exercise his creative gifts. Therein lies a basic distinction between service and play.

Now as it is with faithful service to divine truth, so also is it with faithful service to divine love. Here we take note of a theological conviction that seems to be growing in the Church, that there belongs to the ministry of God in and through the Church not only a vocation of ministers of Word and Sacrament, but also a ministry of diaconal service in the world. The Christian community rightly understanding its mission of service, wills to express itself corporately in loving service to God in meeting human need. And this not simply within the Church on behalf of Church members, but also in the world on behalf of the impoverished and dispossessed. Into this ministry too persons are experiencing themselves called by God and are asking the Church to recognize their calling. The content of the service may often be identical with the self-chosen professions of Christians and other men. The form is that of an ordained service determined solely by God.

The Church is a community whose *raison d'être* is found in its willingness to be solely determined by the Word and Spirit of God. She is a community defined by mission. With secular society it is not so, and that not simply by reason of sin, but even by divine intent. For secular society is a sphere intended for play. Not that play as such is inimical to the Church. Far from it, some views of the Christian life notwithstanding. For the Church in accord with God's intention for man, wills man's freedom for play as that which its own service of God provides a basis for. But, as we have sought to indicate, it is all important to distinguish in an ordered Christian life freedom for service and freedom for play. And the Church is the community where freedom in and for service rules supreme. It is the community whose life is determined solely by God. The Church is the servant of God to whom witness to his truth and action in accord with the uniqueness of his love is made.

The truth to which she serves as witness, that is constitutive of her being and determinative of her life, is God in his self-revelation. It is absolutely unique truth to which man has no other access than the ministry of the Church. There are other kinds of truth of great importance for the quality of human life of which the Church is not necessarily the bearer and certainly not the sole custodian. For truth, no more than being, is identical with God. There is truth that is identical with God whose name is Jesus. "I am the Truth", he says in true apostolic self-testimony. But there is also truth and knowledge of the world and of man in the world of which he is not object or origin, truth and knowledge the discovery of which belongs to man in play. Of course if men play as Christians they will play to God's glory and all that they do will be accompanied by praise. The truth they celebrate and rejoice in will of course be the gospel but it will also be the truth the gospel frees men for. The peculiar calling of the Church is to be witness to truth that is identical with the gospel and that is entirely outside man's capacity to discover or create.

Moreover, there is the uniqueness of love that the Church is called to know and serve. It is a love beyond all man's natural capacity to know or to perform. "Wherefore, be ye imitators of God and walk in love as Christ has loved you." (Ephesians 5: 1) The Church is called to a life in love in imitation of God, who in Jesus Christ took into fellowship with himself the unworthy, and served in love those who turned upon him in enmity or turned away from him in derision or regret. God alone is the source of the power for such loving; he through Word and Spirit is the sole determiner of men who in freedom love like that.

In human history generally man is free in some important ways to determine who his neighbours are. Within certain limits I am free to choose my friends, my companions, my associates. Within perhaps even more restricted limits, I am free to determine whom I will take for wife. But there is a community wherein I am not free, or should not think myself to be free, to decide who my fellows will be. For that is determined for me by the determining action of God. The Church as community of faith and love is God's creation wherein, like it or not, neighbours are provided by God. Here all questions of empathy, of liking or disliking, of free selection of companions for work or pleasure, are transcended. All distinctions between man and man on natural or historical bases are, though not cancelled, yet superseded in a community that is determined not by the fact that one is male or female, Jew or Greek, bond or free, likeable or unlikeable, wise or foolish, but solely by the Word and the free Spirit of God. God himself determines the members of his family. The Church is not the place where free self-determining decision is the primary thing.

There is, of course, an extension of God's will and work in this regard outside the boundaries of the community of faith, within the world. There too, there is a basic sense in which God determines who my neighbour is, whom I am called to meet in agape-love. For the neighbour is, as Jesus in the parable of the Good Samaritan told us, any man who is near and is in need. Here too, in obedient service of him who is the servant of all, there is a transcending of all questions of liking and disliking, of pleasure or pragmatic efficacy that determine natural choice of companionship. Here I am constrained by God's gift of agape-love simply to accept and meet, as best I can, the claim of the neighbour on me who am called to be a servant of God's love. And even the self-chosen neighbours, my special friends and companions in life, those whom I love with so-called natural forms of loving, are such within a context of grace and truth that makes them too the neighbour God calls on me to love in gracious ways. They too, as I and all men do, stand in constant need of human as well as divine forgiveness, of an accept-ance as fellow human beings that underlies all differentiating characteristics that distinguish man from man.

It could be that we are simply stumbling about here over traditional distinctions between nature and grace. Even so I think we have in the process gained some insight into the proper ordering of things as seen from the perspective of God's intention for man. From these perspectives grace does not simply renew and/or perfect nature; it also is the liberating context within which nature is set free to be itself. Grace, as the determination of human existence by God, mediated through the service of the Church, is the God-ordained source of freedom in service and the God-ordained context of man's freedom for play. For play too belongs to God's intention for man. In the story of creation, after having given man being and addressed to him a gracious word as ground and context of all his human life, God turned man's attention toward the world as God's gift to him and called him to the creative task of humanizing his life within it. So the Church as agent of God's continuing address to man of the Word of his forgiving and renewing love, calls man to freedom and sets him free for play. "I am come", says Jesus, "that you may have life, and have it in all its abundance." (cf. S.Jn. 10:10)

How shall we say it rightly? Jesus Christ is at the heart of my being as Christian man. He alone is God's forgiveness and power for life over sin and death. He is my true humanity without whom I, or any man, cannot come to be man in the image of God. He calls me to receive and abide in his Truth and to pour out my life in the humble service of love that he inspires. But as such Jesus does not himself constitute the whole being or meaning of being human in the world. He is one without whom there is no power to be human in the world, the servant whose whole service was to set men free. But he did not himself actualize every capacity for being human for which he sets us free. He did not actualize man's power for being human in every sense — as husband or wife, bearer of children, father or mother; he did not in any significant sense realize man's capacities for cultural creativity as musician, painter, poet, architect. The human capacities for scientific understanding and mastery of nature he did not realize, though he did manifest himself as Lord of nature and human history in the eschatological sense. It is too narrow a Christological understanding of the vocation of man in relation to God that leads a theologian like Ellul to deny that the exercise of human powers in knowing, creating, mastering things in human ways belongs to the original intention of God for man and to affirm that which becomes accept-able in any fashion only through the grace of the forgiveness of man's sin. For in the original beginning, which is Creation, as in the restored beginning, which is Jesus Christ, it was and is not so. God disclosed to Adam that man was made for play.[11] And God in Jesus renewed for Adam his lost vocation. He released man from the guilt and power of sin and gave him freedom for an abundant life. So he announces the good news through the witnessing words of the apostle: "All things are yours, for you are Christ's and Christ is God's." (I Cor. 3: 21-23) It is this theme we wish to explore more fully in our next chapter.

FOOTNOTES

1   See *inter alia, The Book of Common Order of The Church of Scotland,* London, Oxford University Press, 1940, p. 271.

2   Jacques Ellul, *The Meaning of the City*, tr. by Dennis Pardee, Grand Rapids, W. B. Eerdmans, 1970.

3   *Ibid*, p. 113.

4   Karl Barth, *op. cit.*, Volume IV, Part 4, p. 30.

5   *Ibid*, p. 72.

6   See Paul Tillich, *The Protestant Era*, Chicago, University of Chicago Press, 1948, p. 57.

7   cf. Karl Barth, *From Rousseau to Ritschl*, London, S.C.M. Press, 1959, pp. 46-51.

8   cf. Karl Barth, "Wolfgang Amadeus Mozart" in *Religion and Culture: Essays in Honor of Paul Tillich*, ed. Walter Leibrecht, New York, Harper and Bros., 1959, p. 63.

9   *Ibid*, p. 64. I seem to remember that the original formulation to which Barth makes reference here was somewhat closer to the way I have put it but unfortunately I do not remember the original source.

10   See Jeremiah 1: 4-10; Hosea 1: 2; Amos 7: 14-15; S. Jn. 15: 16; II Cor. 3: 5-6, et cetera.

11   See Genesis 1: 28; 2: 18-19.

CHAPTER 5

PLAY

We have been led from the opening chapter through the others in the series to the irresistible conclusion that God has willed for man, in the context of his own self-determining presence and action in human life, freedom to accomplish a human work of self-determination. It seems most fitting to call this latter work, in distinction from service, play. Such a distinction of course is not one between human acts that are done in accordance with God's will and acts that have no reference to it. If the latter were so, it would indeed be that all man's attempts to take responsibility for his life and to accomplish a human work with a sense of joy in self-achievement would be virtually rebellion against God. But we find ourselves led to speak here of the humanizing of life that God himself has willed for man and for which, in creation and redemption, he makes man free. It is the measure of God's self-giving love that he should not will to be the sole determiner of all that happens on the creaturely level of being. Greek gods, maybe, but not the God of Christian faith, are jealous of the creativity of man. The way man provokes the jealousy of God is not by human use of freedom in performing self-determined finite tasks but in the abuse of freedom which seeks to set the self in place of God as author and origin of man's power to be free. God will allow no other gods, self-established or established by man, to challenge his being as Lord. If man himself challenges this prerogative of God, God reacts in judging wrath, albeit a wrath itself strangely born of love. He who seeks to play God, not being God, sins and dies. But he who being man seeks to be *man* of play has both the divine blessing and the divine enablement.

There are theologians who have thought it necessary to interpret God's loving will for man to take responsibility for his own life as being possible only through God's own will to die. There is a divine *kenosis* wherein God's becoming man reaches its extremity in God's own death in Jesus. This it is believed is the Christian message of incarnation, death and resurrection. God dies that man might live. For so long as God is there as man's Other his humanity will inevitably, in one way or another, be seriously qualified if not lost altogether in its relation to God.[1] There is here a kind of belief in the humanification of God, a Hegelian-like antithesis to doctrines of the deification of man. As antidote to the dehumanizing consequences of the latter some find it justified. It asserts in the name of humanity a need for freedom, not simply as a matter of pride but as acknowledgement of a good that is well in accord with God's loving intention for man. But the remedy proposed for the loss of man's humanity is in itself impossible and is not needed when Christian truth is rightly understood. There is no sense, even mythologically, in which the Creator and Redeemer God can be said to die. The death God dies in Jesus is man's death. The resurrection life of Jesus is man's resurrection life. It is indeed human life God gives, restores and preserves in Jesus. But God's own death would mean the death of everything. If the choice were necessary, we would have to take the side of those who identify God with Being against those who speak of God's death. There is no being or power to be apart from God. Originally and continuously in creation, restoratively in redemption, fulfillingly in the end, God gives to all the power to be. But in view of the human consequences of theologians that identify being and God wherein all things finite in the end are lost in the infinity of God, we can symphathize with the intention of those who understand God's love for man in terms of God's will to die that man might live humanly free. And the freedom for which God dies a human death in Jesus does indeed include freedom for play. That for faith makes play a matter of tremendous significance in the life of man.

Play in this perspective is not simply an alternative to work — as though work were service and play were the respite needed by frail, finite man to make renewed and better efforts at service possible. Nor is play a way of speaking humbly of our life of service when compared to the incomparable work of service that is that of Christ the Lord.[2] Play is neither substitute for service nor a means that simply serves the end of service. It is a singular form of work, a way of being human, along with the service God has willed for man. Play is the activity man performs when within the context of a life of faith and love he uses the creative gifts God gives to perform a human work of self-accomplishment with the freedom for so working that God provides. This accomplishment is what constitutes human culture and civilization. It includes science, art, morality and religion. These are in principle what are implied in God's mandate to Adam to name the animals, to take possession of the world and subdue it. Man is set free to acquire a human knowledge of the world, a human appreciation and mastery of it. Science, art and religion, each is a complex intermingling of objective knowledge and imaginative interpretation. In thus knowing the world man is not called to seek for God as if he were inscribed, represented or suggested there. Man may, if he is so gifted by nature, find a "rumour of angels"[3] as he reflects on things. For nature, as we asserted earlier, has a dimension of mystery that may be known by man. Angels are symbols for that dimension of mystery, and as such may form part of the language man uses in witness to God. But the call to exercise freedom in humanizing the world does not intend the sacramental endeavour to read the world as if it were the objectifying expression of the mind of God. It is to know it in its creaturely being and meaning and to use it in ways that are humanly good. Justice to nature requires acknowledgement of what nature is and, with its own limited kinds of freedom, has become. Man must be imitator of God in this, that his lordship over creation is informed by love; and love is "just" to the nature of things. Thus, use of nature should never spell abuse. It occurs to me that the same dialectical interrelation of service and play that God seeks in his relation to man, man should also seek in his relation to nature. Nature is made to serve man in man-determined ways and in that service fulfils a paramount purpose for which it has been made. But nature must also be regarded as standing free of man, free to be itself in natural ways. And it could be that only insofar as man's loving concern for nature's own integrity accompanies his will and intention to make use of it will the latter be a humanly good and justifiable use and not abuse. I have not explored, and do not now have the time to explore, the implications of this train of thought for answering extremely difficult questions that are now in sight concerning e.g., the morality of genetic engineering and the like, to which we will return in our next chapter. But at least we can say that some restraints on man's freedom to manipulate and control nature must come from that other more basic form of freedom which is freedom to do justly and to love.

We have said that morality too belongs to the activity of play, to that which man accomplishes in an exercise of self-determination with a freedom given by God. As God gives power to his creation to fulfil itself in naturally good ways, so God gives man the power to fulfil himself as a creature, to accomplish the moral good. Sometimes Christian men and women are inclined to interpret man's moral goodness, when they would not other kinds of goodness, pantheistically. We should rather see in man's accomplishment of moral goodness something analogous, at the human level of being, to the blossoming and bearing fruit of trees. No more than we interpret the latter as immediate expression of the presence and action of God realizing himself in natural beauty and creativity, should we interpret the moral acts of man in such a way. Both are the actualization of powers of being God gave and gives to his creation thus both actualizing themselves in natural ways. It is creation, at creaturely levels of being, actualizing freely powers for goodness that God gave initially, and sustains continuously, that results both in the beauty, creativity and usefulness of the blossoming, fruit-bearing of trees and in the being and deed of the good man. We know, of course, and will have to take serious account of the fact, that the good creation of God is actually riddled with evil and man made for the free exercise of goodness is actually sinner. Everything in nature and human history is marked by darkness and death. Everything in nature is open to disease and doomed to decay. The moral achievements of the good man are corrupted by the sin which seeks the self's own good against God and the neighbour so that man uses even moral goodness as occasion for pride and self-seeking. Yet, by virtue of the constancy of God's loving will and forgiving love for all that he has made, his creation still possesses freedom for good, even if extremely qualified.

Religion I have interpeted as man's experience and creative account of the mystery that belongs to creation itself. Religion, no more than science, art or morality, has to do directly with God. Of course, as we have said, the language of religion, like the language of morality, art or science, or even that used by man in the language of everyday communication of man with man, can be used to bear witness to God, the Wholly Other, who names himself in special deeds. But in itself, religion, like art with which it may have much in common, belongs to culture — to the free exercise of man's creative capacities for knowing, interpreting, using creation's gifts. Religion knows and interprets nature at the level of mystery, disclosed in experiences of wonder and awe. It seems to me wrong to find as some do the origin of religion and art in man's hunger for God, in an eros-longing born of a lost or yet to be found infinity.[4] Religion and art may indeed become an idolatrous substitute for God and passion for the infinite may become the source or consequence of sin. But, in principle, in accord with the intention of God, they are not so. It may be too, as Berdyaev says, that art is full of symbols of another world.[5] But the other world is to our thinking not that of an eternity in some way identical with the Being of God, but is rather a dimension of this world, symbolized as "heaven", seen, known, expressed aesthetically or religiously.

If to play belong these multi-faceted exercises of human power God in gracious love provides man freedom for, there are still many questions to ask about their relations one with the other and their relations in common with the grace of God. The life of faith is an ordered life and one effect of its ordering is the refusal to allow any one or other activity of the spirit of man the right to make an exclusive claim. Scientism, moralism, aestheticism, religiosity — all result from a disordered understanding of the meaning of life, its purpose and end, and therefore of the human spirit and its calling; and all are questioned and negated by faith in God. Faith and its gifts restores wholeness to one's human way of being and to one's view of its achievements and possibilities. The moralist, who asserts the moral claim, as if it exhausted the vocation of human spirit in its freedom for self-determination, is called by faith into question in the name of the fuller freedom God wills for man. The religious man who asserts finality for his vision of the world and regards man's vocation as the all-absorbing quest for its attainment, is challenged by the reality of God and the fulness of the freedom he intends. In the freedom for play, any individual may, in the freedom of self-determining choice, will to give himself in limiting vocation to the cultivation of one or other of the expressions of the human spirit and seek thereby to make a more significant contribution to the fulfilment of the humanity of man. But, in principle, other ways of actualizing a free spirit are open to him, and are certainly open to others who choose in life another vocation than his. What is one man's vocation may well be another's avocation in the freedom of play. And we remember that all expressions of play take place within the limits of love without which man and all his accomplishments are nothing worth.[6]

In this regard we must confess that man's freedom for play is severely qualified. Man's is a mortally wounded spirit, one whose being and work in all its aspects bear the marks of vanity and death. Ellul is not wrong in interpreting man's building of cities as shot through with signs of rebellion against God and riddled with dire consequences of that rebellion. Ellul is only wrong in regarding the creative enterprise of man as in itself an act of sin. In *fact* culture and civilization may be a tower of Babel built by man in contesting God. But in *principle,* (that is, in accordance with God's *intent*), it is not so.

We have noted before that Ellul's mistake may be due to a reading off of man's essential nature and work from what in fact he has become and made of it through sin and of mistakenly reading off God's original and unchanging intention for man from his gracious rescue-operation of reconciliation, bringing life out of death. We believe to find other things concerning God's intention for man in the scriptural witness to his self-revealed Word. There witness is made to God's will for man's freedom for self-determining being and act, always of course within the context of God's own Lordly being and doing and a recognition of the fact that he alone is freedom's source. It is because God is not acknowledged in these ways that man and his works take on the grim aspect that Ellul rightly sees them wear. God stands in judgment against the pride of man that will not acknowledge him as God. We hear his word of judgment in the witnessing words of the apostle: "For it is written, I will destroy the wisdom of the wise, and bring to nothing the understanding of the prudent ... Hath God not made foolish the wisdom of this world." (I Cor. 1: 18-20) The cross of Jesus Christ casts its dark shadow across the whole of man's cultural enterprise. The God who as man suffered death at the hands of religious, moral, cultured men, says "No" to the pride and rebellion that say "No" to him and to his will for faith and love as context for all the other forms of our being and doing as men. God wills indeed to say "Yes" to the culture that is simply, yet wonderfully, man's attempt to discover and realize all the dimensions of his humanity. We hear that "Yes" to all aspects of life that are good in another word of the same apostle: "Finally, brethren, whatever is true, whatever is honourable, whatever is just, whatever is pure, whatever is lovely, whatever is gracious, if there is any excellence, if there is anything worthy of praise, think about these things." (Philippians 4: 8) However, for man the sinner, culture becomes inevitably an attempt at self-salvation, an attempt at self-recovery of a centre that he has lost. All such attempts but leave man fast in his egocentricity. Eccentrically, he sets himself at the centre in place of God. Culture thus becomes a proud assertion of man against God. Man in selfish self-centredness pretends that all power and authority for being human derive from self. So his autonomy, his God-willed freedom for self-expression, is transformed into an occasion for betrayal rather than for believing response. God, therefore, must address a word of judgment against man. And, being Lord of history, his judgment becomes incorporate in man's historical life. Enlightened by faith, we can read off from history judgment and the consequence of sin. T. S. Eliot has done so and in his chorus from *The Rock* tells us what he has found there in a modern word of prohetic warning:

"O weariness of men who turn from God
To the grandeur of your mind and the glory of your action,
To arts and inventions and daring enterprises,
To schemes of human greatness thoroughly discredited,
Binding the earth and water to your service,
Exploiting the seas and developing the mountains,
Dividing the stars into common and preferred,
Engaged in devising the perfect refrigerator,
Engaged in working out a rational morality,
Engaged in printing as many books as possible,
Plotting of happiness and flinging empty bottles,
Turning from your vacancy to fevered enthusiasm
For nation or race or what you call humanity;
Though you forget the way to the Temple,
There is one who remembers the way to your door:
Life you may evade, but Death you shall not.
You shall not deny the Stranger."[7]

The words are apt for what has happened because men have substituted culture for God and God rejects the substitution. However, this word of judgment, of refusal, is not, thank God, the final word God speaks. He comes in his incarnate Son to speak in history a word of forgiveness and new life in freedom for man. "God was in Christ reconciling the world to himself." (II Cor. 5: 19)

"We have to learn over and over again, that the Word of God is a
word of death, not in relation to the foundation intention of the
humanity of man, but in regard to its historical pretentions."[8]

The quotation from Ricoeur gives us opportunity to repeat our thesis: we have been set within a world of God's creating, and given power and authority by the Author of all, to discover and actualize to the full powers of self-achievement. As in the bible story of creation, God gives man a mandate to build a human world within the world of his creating, in unchanging love giving to him initially, and sustaining in him, freedom for the task. All that is asked of man — and that too is grace — is that he should cultivate his human gifts in trusting love and gratitude to his Creator and in loving companionship with fellow-man.

"Our God," says Ricoeur again, "is a God-Act, a God-Gift, who makes man a creator in his turn in the measure in which he receives and is willing to receive the gift of being free."[9]

And when man, through his refusal, through his betrayal of the gift of being free, lost freedom to be joyfully, trustingly, thankfully, creative and became incapable of being or doing anything that did not bear the mark of vanity and death, God, in an amazing fidelity of love and constancy of intention, came to man, as Man among men, to restore to him his freedom, to win for him victory over sin and death. Bonhoeffer has understood it so well. In these majestic themes of the gospel — of incarnation, death and resurrection, and the second coming of the Christ — we find a charter of freedom for human life and work. For Bonhoeffer, in his beautiful metaphor from music, they provide the ground bass, the *cantus firmus*, for a counterpoint, a polyphony of human life in freedom, of man engaged in being human in the world.[10]

Here in the gospel of God's grace we find expressed the heart-centre of a renewed attempt to live human life in accordance with the intention of God, with resources that supersede those which in creation God provides. His gifts of forgiveness and new life in Christ now provide the source of freedom for a filled-out human life. The eschatological promise of life's fulfilment in God's kingdom through God's victory over sin and death, as witnessed in the scriptures, includes all that is good which man and nature realize. As we shall see in our next chapter it provides the new horizon for human life in time.

We are not permitted to think that in Jesus Christ man, and through man nature too, have been elevated to a new dimension of being through ontic union of God with man in him. It is indeed true that the grace God grants to man in creation to be and to become human is even more abounding in the grace of God's redemption which is his forgiving, liberating Word. But this original intention for man in creation has not thereby been superseded but rather renewed with a promise of fulfilment in his gracious deed of redemption. The life that he came in Jesus to give us abundantly was the filled-out human life he willed for us in the beginning. The things that are added to those who seek first God's kingdom and his righteousness in Jesus are things man needs to make and keep life human in the world. That these will be made available in abundance to every man in need, in a world that man is made free by love to dominate, is the meaning of the promise that is given in the Bible about nature's and history's End. The good that nature mourns in Paul's witness to her bondage[11] is, as Tillich says,[12] a "lost" good, not the infinite longing for the not-yet attained good of the creature's union with God. To be released from the bondage of evil, that in the end spells death for everything, means to be released for the human life God willed in the beginning.

There is a true and a false way of understanding the truth to which the hymn-writer gives moving expression:

"Thou, O Christ, art all I want,
More than all in Thee I find."[13]

As witness to the fact that all good gifts of God are renewed to man, even as they are transcended in the forgiveness that he in Jesus Christ provides, the words are true.   As witness to the unqualified nature of the human spirit's commitment to Jesus Christ in faith and love they express truly God's will and our calling.   But as a pious expression of a way of being in Christ that robs human life of its many-sided dimensions of being human in the world, the sentiment is profoundly called in question by God's fuller word. "All things are yours, for you are Christ's and Christ is God's."   "I am come that ye might have life and have it more abundantly."   "Seek first God, and his kingdom — in Jesus — and all other things that are good will be added unto you."   "If the Son shall make you free, you are free indeed" — free for all that is human and humanly good.[14]   We have already said it, and I hope said it without profanity and without offence: Jesus as True Man, and New Man, in himself does not actualize every power of being human in the world. He is indeed the source of all our capacity for being genuinely human in the world.   He, as agape-love, is a power liberating eros, as Alvez has said, by which many kinds and dimensions of human creativity are actualized.   He came to be the Saviour of all men from bondage to sin and death.   He came to set men free.   He is the centre and the circumference of all our life in God.

We have noted that in the theology of Karl Rahner there are times when he draws back from the full implications of a theology that goes unqualifiedly in the direction of the deification of man — the filling up of our human finitude with the infinity of God, finally realized in the beatific vision.   We find Rahner's hesitation in the name of a loved humanity once more expressed in this quotation in which he thinks again about human deification finally fulfilled in the beatific vision wherein God becomes "all in all":

"One will perhaps give a pious thought to the consideration (not, of course, in dogmatic theology) that 'besides' the *visio beatifica* (in which every other knowledge and beatitude is given supereminently, so that one does not really see what else could still be of interest) one might still be able to derive an 'accidental' joy from the humanity of Christ in heaven."[15]

The truth of the matter is, I believe there should be — will be — nothing 'accidental' about our fulfilled joy in Christ's humanity.   It is the fulfilment of God's loving will for man, together with *everything* human that Christ's humanity serves.

FOOTNOTES

1   cf. Thomas J. J. Altizer, *The Gospel of Christian Atheism*, Philadelphia, West-minster Press, 1966; and in *Radical Theology and the Death of God*, coeditor, William Hamilton, Indianapolis, Bobbs-Merrill, 1966.

2   cf. Karl Barth, *Church Dogmatics*, Volume III, Part 4, pp. 520-564 where, in a section entitled "Freedom for Life", Barth interprets play in both these ways.

3   The phrase is suggested of course by the book of Peter Berger that bears this title, in which Berger speaks of "transcendence". For him "signals of transcend-ence" noted in modern culture are thought to "signal God" the "supernatural". In our understanding, "signals of transcendence" signify nature's own mysterious depths. It is here that Tillich's "self-transcending naturalism" has its place. But surely the truly "supernatural" is not rumoured by angels but declared in God's self-revealing Word. See Peter Berger, *A Rumour of Angels: modern society and the rediscovery of the supernatural,* Garden City, Doubleday, 1969; *The Theology of Paul Tillich,* eds. Charles W. Kegley & Robert W. Bretall, New York, Macmillan, 1956, chapter "Reply to Interpretation and Criticism" by Paul Tillich, p. 341.

4   cf. Karl Rahner, *op. cit.,* Volume III, 1967, pp. 316-317.

5   "L'art est plein de symboles d'un autre monde." N. Berdyaev, *Dialectique Exist-entielle Du Dieu et de l'Humain,* Paris, J.-B. Janin, 1947, p. 179.

6   cf. I Cor. 13.

7   T. S. Eliot, "Choruses from 'The Rock'", in *Collected Poems, 1909-1935,* London, Faber & Faber, 1936, p. 167.

8   I regret that I do not know the source of this quotation from the writings of Paul Riceour. I noted it, and the following quotation, years ago. Memory of the source fails me.

9   See footnote 8.

10   cf. Dietrich Bonhoeffer, *Letters and Papers from Prison,* ed. by Eberhard Bethge, 3rd edition revised and enlarged, London, S.C.M. Press, 1967, pp. 162-163; also p. 156.

11   Romans 8: 20-21.

12   See Paul Tillich "Nature Also Mourns for a Lost Good" in *The Shaking of the Foundations,* New York, Scribner, 1948, p. 76.

13   The words, of course, are from the well-known hymn of Charles Wesley, "Jesus Lover of my soul".

14   The quotations are in sequence from I Cor. 3: 21-23; S. Jn. 10: 10; S. Mtt. 6: 33; S. Jn. 8: 36.

15   Karl Rahner, *op. cit.,* Volume III, 1967, p. 44.

CHAPTER 6

HISTORY AND ESCHATOLOGY

It is an inescapable conclusion of doctrines affirmed earlier that man's historical existence cannot be thought to be unwarranted, fortuitous or even of secondary significance from the perspective of God's intention for man. Indeed, an historical mode of existence is that at which all of God's work on behalf of man aims. God makes and remakes man for history even to the extent of himself entering into man's historical life. In thinking of human history from the standpoint of faith emphasis must be placed on its futurity. Past and present are of profound significance. But the present borrows meaning from the future that the past promises and that the present seeks to fulfil. The person and work of Jesus Christ both fulfil and recreate the promise given by the prophet Jeremiah:

> "For I know the plans I have for you, says the Lord; plans for welfare and not evil, to give you a future and a hope." (Jeremiah 29: 11)

The flight of the arrow of faith of which we spoke in our first chapter is directed toward the future. As we said earlier, the "downward and upward" point of view of many traditional theologies does not give an accurate account of God's intention for man if our understanding of the matter is correct. The descent of God into human history is not for purposes of returning man in gnostic, or any other fashion, to some other-worldly life with God. We do not understand history from the perspective of faith as Rahner does when he speaks of " ... the faith which knows that entry into God's eternity can be gained through all the exits of the history of the world. ..."[1] Historical existence is not a mode of life from which God wills that man escape; and to enter into God's eternity in Rahner's sense is not the destiny God intends for man. Charles West states it accurately when he says: "It is not the eternal but the future toward which life moves."[2] Nor is "the future toward which life moves" to be thought of as the fulfilment of the process whereby human life becomes progressively sacramentalized, as if human history generally and also nature, come to be more and more a locus for manifestation of God. Karl Rahner in what seems to me an alternate yet also questionable way of looking at history to that cited above, asks

> "whether there might not be a formula for saving history as God's progressive taking possession of the world of history, as the manifestation, ever clearer and more hidden at once, of God in the

world as his quasi-sacramental *mysterium*. The Christ would appear as the summit of this history, and Christology as its sharpest formulation, just as inversely saving history would appear as the prelude and extension of Christ's own history."[3]

It is not surprising to find Rahner developing this sort of sacramentalist view of history out of theological positions we have seen him adopting earlier. But it is surprising to find similar, though by no means identical views in a theological work that at first seemed to offer radically different possibilities. I am thinking of Harvey Cox in his "The Secular City".[4]   Beginning with a thesis that, (given the title of the book), should have led to a radical secularization of man's historical existence, Cox actually, or so it seems to me, ends with a "religious" view of history as primarily determined by God.   For him too history is primarily God's achievement — not just the history which is God's accomplishment in Jesus, but history generally.   For it too is that wherein God is thought of as the primary actor and through which he mediates his grace to man.   From this perspective universal history is salvation history.   For Cox, Jesus Christ comes to men not primarily through the proclamation of the gospel of a unique history in which God was self-involved in the existence of man, but rather through the processes of history generally, through social change and political action.   Through these God performs his work in the here-and-now of man's historical life.   The Church's task for Cox is not primarily fidelity to witness to God's disclosure through redemptive action in the history of Jesus, which witness serves to enable God to be redemptively present here and now.   Rather, Cox calls the Church first of all to discern what God is presently doing in the world as primary agent of social change:

> "Jesus Christ comes to his people not primarily through ecclesiastical traditions, but through social change ... Canon and tradition function not as sources of revelation but as precedents by which present events can be checked out as the possible loci of God's action."[5]

Cox does come to say in his book that God "insists on turning the world over to man as his responsibility,"[6] and he does explore what that might mean.   But much of what he says in the final chapter, and elsewhere in the concluding section of the book, seems to me to state the contrary.   "Theology today", he writes, "must be that reflection-in-action by which the Church finds out what this politican-God is up to and moves in to work along with him."[7]   Or again: "God comes to us today in events of social change, in what theologians have often called *history*, but what we call *politics*."[8] Is this not after all a "religious" view of history?   Why is the city called a "secular city", when the primary actor in its creation is the one Cox calls the "politican God"? Here there would seem to be no room for play — for human self-determining action — only for service, the responding action of man to the action of God. This is indicated by the fact that Cox speaks of a *"theology* of social change", a *"theology* of revolution", which for him take precedence over a "theology of revelation."[9] It is hard now to see the consistency in Cox's choice, in the first section of his book, of Barth over Tillich when surely it is more in accord with Tillich to speak of a theology of culture as preceding a theology of the biblical Word.

In the introduction to Rubem Alves' book "A Theology of Human Hope", Harvey Cox mentions criticisms addressed by Alves to his "The Secular City", even with regard to his theology of social change. Cox acknowledges the accuracy of some of the criticism, though "luckily mostly on notions about which I have changed by mind".[10] Cox does not say whether the change in mind includes a wholehearted acceptance of Alves' messianic humanism which indeed is more radically humanistic than the "religious" views of Cox described above. In any event, Alves develops with a more radical consistency what is implied in Cox's phrase "God insists on turning the world over to man as his responsibility".

Alves' book is the most recent I have read on a Christian understanding of history. I find in its concern for the realization of man's freedom to determine what belongs to his destiny as willed by God much that is in harmony with my understanding of God's intention for man. However, for reasons developed earlier, I nonetheless find that Alves' theology is reductionist in its end result. He allows the present historical moment too much control over the biblical Word. In our introduction we spoke of the importance of allowing the biblical Word to be addressed by questions that arise out of the historical moment but always in such a way that they are answered out of the gospel so that it is afforded primacy as God's Word to man. Alves moves too far in the direction of transforming theology into anthropology by his insistence on speaking of God only in terms of man. He thereby finally does full justice to neither. To speak of God simply as an experience of grace without a name that gives birth in human history to freedom, newness and a future with hope may be to speak rightly of the effect of God's being and action in relation to man. But it fails to do justice to the wholeness of God's truth. To speak of man as primary agent in effecting social change, especially through political action, may be to speak truly of man's vocation in effecting human good. But it is diminishing in terms of the multi-dimensional character of human life. It fails to do justice to man's relation to God in worship and service and also to other expressions of the human spirit within the realm of play. We can understand how political concerns assert their dominance in the historical situation within which Alves lives and works as Christian humanist. But theology seeks wholeness of being and truth. Surely a "theology of human hope" should allow and offer wider vistas of what God gives man freedom for than confining hope to the domain of political action no matter how existentially important, even primary, the latter may be thought to be.

But let us now turn to our account of the meaning of history and history's end, interpreted in the light of things already said, and of further things to be derived from our understanding of God's intention for man.

Man's historical existence is a complex web of interrelated actions of the spirit of God and the spirit of man that we have described under the rubrics worship, service, play. Such actions are creative of human history. But is that history in its totality to be called universal history or salvation history? Is there a distinction in theological understanding between the two? I think the two are distinguishable yet inseparably interrelated the one with the other.

If by salvation history we mean, as indeed we must, the action whereby God accomplishes the justification of the sinner and the renewal of life in righteousness, we must confess that salvation history lies at the heart of man's universal history and is its circumference as well. What we have testified about God as centre and boundary of human existence is to be given an historical interpretation here. God sought in Israel, on the basis of free election not merit, a community whose existence among the nations of the world would unambiguously point to God as the sovereign, origin and sustainer of all creaturely reality and the source too of freedom to be human in the world. Set in the midst of fallen mankind, the prime mark of whose fallenness was idolatry, Israel's vocation was to honour the one true God through worship and to fulfil the divine command to love. Her history was intended to be salvation history, the manifestation in human history of God's presence and deed, calling men back from the destructive eccentricity of idolatrous life to the acknowledgement of him as the one true God, the world's Creator, and to his service in love as the service in which alone man is truly free. In Israel's history God manifested his glory in opposition to idolatry and brought judgment upon man's failure to love. And in that history too God manifested his glory in words and deeds of forgiveness transcending judgment so that even judgment was seen to be the strange working of his love. This manifestation of God's glory in a history of judgment, and grace transcending judgment, was supremely fulfilled in the human history of Jesus the Christ. Israel, being sinner, and in that being what all men are, did not and could not bear unambiguous witness to God's intention for man. So God's identification with human history became even more intimate than in Israel's history it was. It became as intimate indeed as incarnation, the union of God with man, in the divine-history of Jesus Christ. God's glory was now manifest in a divine love that took judgment upon itself, in a human love that willed to accept that judgment and its consequence. Out of this history that was at once that of God and man came forgiveness, a new life in love and freedom to be man.

Now the presence and action of God in the human history of Israel —

Jesus Christ cannot be regarded, I believe, as a particular instance of God's general presence and action in the universal history of mankind. Salvation history is not simply a term to be used for God present and active anywhere or everywhere. It may indeed be true that the comprehensive term to be used for the sum and substance of God's action on behalf of man is "freedom": freedom for faith, freedom for love, freedom for fulfilment of all man's capacities for being human in the world. But this life in freedom is an ordered life, as we have tried to show. Freedom for play is grounded in the freedom of service, and service in the freedom of faith and love. And all are comprehended by that free grace that is God's forgiveness of sin. One knows nothing rightly about God's presence and action in the world if he does not know that it proceeds from the forgiving grace that is actualized and made manifest in the cross and resurrection of Jesus. That is why the mission of the Church, both as creature and servant of the gospel of forgiveness, cannot be regarded as secondary to any other mission of God within the world. No "theology of social change" or "theology of revolution" is primary to a theology of a revealed history of salvation in Israel — Jesus Christ. Social change and revolution are themselves rooted in a complex intermingling of the freedoms of service and play. And both of these forms of freedom are grounded in the basic freedom of forgiveness and new life found in Jesus' triumph over sin's guilt and power. The mission of the Church is not therefore first of all and primarily to seek to discover where and how God is working in the world and then, in the knowledge and power of faith, to identify herself with that working. The mission of the Church is the proclamation of the free grace of forgiveness and the new life in Jesus which is the context in Reality of any other freedom that God gives to man. If man, individually or communally, is to seek on his own responsibility to actualize powers for being human in the world without illusion, as well as without idolatry, he is dependent on the liberating power of the Church's service to truth, the truth of the gospel, as well as the liberating power of the Church's service of love, the agape-love the gospel discloses and imparts. We say again, God despite man's sin, continues in a fidelity of love through his Spirit to work towards freeing man for every kind of being and doing whereby human life is fulfilled. The supreme manifestation of that fidelity, the source of its presence anywhere, is found in the revelation of God's presence and action in Jesus Christ. He alone utters, for he alone is the Word: "I am come that you might have life and have it more abundantly." "Abide in me and I in you for apart from me you can do nothing." "If the Son shall make you free, you are free indeed."[11]

So salvation history is defined as the history whereby God accomplishes the justification of the sinner, the renewal of life in righteousness and its rescue from death. This history is central to and comprehends all God's action in relation to man but it does not exhaust it. His presence and action in the world includes also his presence and work as the creator and preserver of the humanity of man despite sin.   He is providentially present and active as the creative ground of every possibility of man to be and do.   God's kingdom, his sovereign rule in love over all that he has made, has salvation history at its core, even as this history has God's kingdom as its aim and end.   It is not wrong but right for the Church in its service of the gospel of salvation to recognize in faith and love that there are many ways of God's working in the world of which the Church is not the custodian, and many human ways of knowing and serving the human good, of which it is not the source.   These all belong to God's kingdom which the Church's service to the gospel also serves.   There are forms of the service of God that are performed by ministers of God who are not disciples of Jesus Christ.   Service, as we have defined it, is the work that God accomplishes in and through man by virtue of his own presence and inspiration.   When the Church in intercessory prayer beseeches God to give the spirit of wisdom and understanding, of justice and truth, to rulers and servants of the state, it is the preserving and liberating work of God through such service on behalf of which the Church prays.   God is present and at work within the world through his spirit, freeing men to serve his purposes of love.   But such service does not make men Christian, any more than the service of Cyrus made him a believing member of the community of Israel.[12]   Those who perform it are indeed servants of the kingdom of God, human instruments through which God's loving will is accomplished.   But they and their service are in the end subject to the judging, forgiving and renewing love accomplished and made manifest in Jesus Christ.

Therefore, the kingdom of God is at once both less and more extensive than salvation history.   We seek to do justice to this apparent paradox by speaking of salvation history as both the centre and the circumference of all that takes place in the interactions of God with man and man with God.   It is centre, for it accomplishes and declares the forgiving love that is origin and mark of all God's dealings with man.   It is circumference because no service of God through man in the world is perfect and no servant of God survives the ruin of death.   If in the end man's imperfect service is accepted, and the unacceptable servant is renewed out of death, it is because of the forgiveness and new life accomplished in Jesus, the gospel of which it is the mission of the Church to declare.

Within the orbit of God's kingdom that is both less and more than salvation history man's spirit is active in play as well as service.   Play makes its unique contribution to human history — indeed a contribution most crucial in kind.   For to play belong all the determinations of human destiny that derive from the activities of man in the fields of science and the arts.   Who can help but ask today where the exercise of the freedom God wills for and gives to man will take us in the areas of scientific knowledge applied to the mastery and change of nature including man's own?   The political theologies of our time wrestle with the problems of social change through political action in the service of justice and human good generally. And no Christian should deny the crucial importance of such concern. There are equally, if not more crucial questions in terms of the destiny of man, related to the decision man will make with free self-determination in technological fields such, for example, as cybernetics and genetic engineering. A short while ago in human history we were shocked and still are terrified to discover the dimension of the freedom God allows to man in the scientific mastery over nature as found in the discovery and use of nuclear fission. The sense of the tremendous power man has for life or death in that dread discovery is still with us and the consciousness of it will accompany us to history's end. But an equally terrible dimension of human freedom for determining human destiny is now coming into view in terms of the technologies just mentioned.[13]   To what use will man put, to what uses should he put, the power they yield to determine his destiny. We accept that there are limits of freedom for play set by faith in God and love for the neighbour, and by the self-imposed limits of morality, judgments of value and good taste. But within such limits what is acceptable to man?   Does the freedom given to man to make the self-determining choice of how he will use for human ends a given nature include also the freedom to transform life so to speak "unnaturally"? Of course man has no power on his own apart from nature to accomplish anything.   In that he differs from God.   But through novel combinations of natural powers, over which he has considerable control, man has brought and will continue to bring new things into being, both for good and ill.

We cannot simply adopt a negative attitude towards the technological enterprise.   We do not have to agree with Father Arthur Gibson's way of expressing it when he speaks of "the sacrament of technology",[14] to agree with his thesis that there is in technology tremendous possibilities of serving human good.   But what are the limits set by God and love for the neighbour and even man's own decision of what serves the humanity of man, for freedom's exercise in these regards?   And what are the directions our human determination of human destiny should take?

Man himself must work out the answers to these crucial questions.   From a Christian perspective he is called to do so within the context of faith and love.   But he is also permitted to do so within the liberating perspective of hope.   The hope that gives him patient, trusting courage as he "makes history" is both provisional and ultimate in kind.   Provisional hope is grounded in the fact that God's creation though *actually* fallen is *essentially* good, and signs of its good are there to be found in things that are pure, lovely, just and of good report which the Apostle calls us constantly to think upon. (Phil. 4: 8)   May we not as Christians say that there is an indefectibility in nature, analogous to indefectibility in the Church, both having origin in the grace of God?   It is true that all things in nature and man are marred by evil and destined for death.   But lilies do grow, birds still nest, man wears though marred a human face, unsurpassed at times in loveliness, and his spirit always yearns for escape from bondage into freedom and knows enough of goodness to rationalize its evil ways. A provisional hope even better grounded, though also limited and precarious, and thus never ultimate in kind, is found in the effects witness to the Word of God's forgiving love works in the world to heal the human spirit's wound and challenge it to love — effects found even in the thought and life of men who do not acknowledge God. Here too we find a result of the Church's faithful service to God's Word. Not only is the Church founded and built up by the proclamation of the gospel; culture also reaps a benefit.

However these hopes as we have said are only proximate. They are not themselves sufficient to secure the human spirit against despair and allow a peaceful rather than a frantic facing of questions related to human freedom we raised a moment ago. "History", says Moltmann, " ... is first and foremost a relationship to the promised future of God and only then is it a relationship of man to the world and to himself."[15] It is in the promised future of God that ultimate hope lies. Man's spirit of freedom in the world suffers a precariousness born of sin and nature's fallenness which makes any final resting upon provisional hope impossible. Only ultimate hope in the final triumph of God's grace, symbolized for us in Jesus' second coming, can encourage the thoughtful spirit sufficiently to save it from despair.

The fulfilment promised by God in Jesus' victory over sin and death includes all the dimensions of the human spirit and its activities we have mentioned in this series of lectures. In the biblical witness to God's future all are present — worship, service and play: there is ever in the fulfilled kingdom praise offered to God in a presence no longer hidden and known only to faith but rather now manifest to all; there is perfection of love in the kingdom in which then only righteousness dwells; and there is room for play in the kingdom into which the nations are said to bring their glory, which we can only interpret as a future of God in which human culture — human creativity — is given a place.[16]

How far we seem in this vision of the End from ideas of a beatific vision that absorbs into itself the sum total of what it means to be human in the intention of God. How far we are from thoughts of deification that regard man's being as simply a finite stage for playing out a drama of the divine life, as though finally only the Creator and not the creature could be real and good. Rahner need not have hesitantly and apologetically, speculated whether it might not be possible to take "pious note" of the possibility of having in heaven, "besides" the beatific vision, an "accidental joy" in the humanity of Christ.[17] For in giving himself to man — such is the mystery and wonder of his love — God has willed to give man to himself to fulfil his creaturehood in a polyphony of spirit expressed of course in worship and service, but (for that too is God's good pleasure) also most assuredly in play.

FOOTNOTES

1 Karl Rahner, *op. cit.*, Volume V, 1956, p. 113.
2 Charles West, *op. cit.*, p. 72.
3 Karl Rahner, *op. cit.*, Volume I, 1961, pp. 166-167.
4 Harvey Cox, *The Secular City*, New York, Macmillan, 1965.
5 *Ibid*, pp. 147-148.
6 *Ibid*, p. 259.
7 *Ibid*, p. 255.
8 *Ibid*, p. 261.
9 See *ibid*, Chapter 5, "Towards a Theology of Social Change", pp. 105 ff.
10 See Rubem Alves, *A Theology of Human Hope*, Washington/Cleveland, Corpus Books, 1969, p. xii.
11 The quotations are, respectively, from S. Jn. 10: 10; 15: 45; 8: 36.
12 Isaiah 44: 28; 45:1 ff.
13 For a description of some of the rather frightening possibilities alluded to here see Gerald Leach, *The Biocrats*, Pelican Books, 1972.
14 *The Ecumenist*, Volume II, No. 6, September-October, 1973, pp. 92-97.
15 J. Moltmann, *Hope and Planning*, London, S.C.M., 1971, p. 18.
16 See the scriptural references in footnote 9 of Chapter 1.
17 See Chapter 5, footnote 15.

SUPPLEMENTS

1. FOOTNOTES TO A THEOLOGY
The Karl Barth Colloquium of 1972

Edited and with an Introduction by
MARTIN RUMSCHEIDT

1974
ISBN 0-919812-02-3

149 pp.
$3.50 (paper)

2. MARTIN HEIDEGGER'S PHILOSOPHY OF RELIGION
JOHN R. WILLIAMS

1977
ISBN 0-919812-03-1

198 pp.
$4.00 (paper)

3. MYSTICS AND SCHOLARS
The Calgary Conference on Mysticism 1976

Edited by
HAROLD COWARD
and
TERENCE PENELHUM

1977
ISBN 0-919812-04-X

viii + 118 pp.
$4.00 (paper)

4. GOD'S INTENTION FOR MAN
Essays in Christian Anthropology
WILLIAM O. FENNELL

1977
ISBN 0-919812-05-8

vi + 56 pp.
$2.50 (paper)

Available from:

WILFRID LAURIER UNIVERSITY PRESS
Wilfrid Laurier University
Waterloo, Ontario, Canada N2L 3C5

EDITIONS

1. LA LANGUE DE YA'UDI

Description et classement de l'ancien parler de Zencirli dans le cadre des langues sémitiques du nord-ouest

PAUL EUGENE DION, o.p.

1974
ISBN 0-919812-01-5

509 pp.
$4.50 (paper)

STUDIES IN RELIGION / SCIENCES RELIGIEUSES
Revue canadienne / A Canadian Journal

Abonnements / Subscriptions

Abonnement personnel: $10.00 (quatre fascicules)
Abonnement pour les institutions: $15.00 (quatre fascicules)
Fascicule isolé : $4.00

Individual subscriptions: $10.00 (four issues)
Institutional subscriptions: $15.00 (four issues)
Individual issues: $4.00

ISSN 0008-4298

Tout chèque doit être fait à l'ordre de Wilfrid Laurier University Press.
Make cheques payable to Wilfrid Laurier University Press

WILFRID LAURIER UNIVERSITY PRESS
Wilfrid Laurier University
Waterloo, Ontario, Canada N2L 3C5

DATE DUE
